Reliable Reasoning

The Jean Nicod Lectures
François Recanati, editor

Reliable Reasoning

Induction and Statistical Learning Theory

Gilbert Harman and Sanjeev Kulkarni

A Bradford Book
The MIT Press
Cambridge, Massachusetts
London, England

© 2007 Massachusetts Institute of Technology

MIT Press books may be purchased at special quantity discounts for business or sales promotional use. For information, please email special_sales@mitpress.mit.edu or write to Special Sales Department, The MIT Press, 55 Hayward Street, Cambridge, MA 02142.

This book was set in Stone Serif and Stone Sans on 3B2 by Asco Typesetters, Hong Kong, and was printed and bound in the United States of America.

Library of Congress Cataloging-in-Publication Data

Harman, Gilbert.
Reliable reasoning : induction and statistical learning theory / Gilbert Harman and Sanjeev Kulkarni.
    p.   cm. — (The Jean Nicod lectures)
"A Bradford book."
Includes bibliographical references and index.
ISBN 978-0-262-08360-7 (hardcover : alk. paper)
1. Reasoning. 2. Reliability. 3. Induction (Logic). 4. Computational learning theory. I. Kulkarni, Sanjeev. II. Title.
BC177.H377   2007
161—dc22   2006033527

10   9   8   7   6   5   4   3   2   1

Contents

Series Foreword

The Jean Nicod Lectures are delivered annually in Paris by a leading philosopher of mind or philosophically oriented cognitive scientist. The 1993 inaugural lectures marked the centenary of the birth of the French philosopher and logician Jean Nicod (1893–1931). The lectures are sponsored by the Centre National de la Recherche Scientifique (CNRS), in cooperation with the Ecole des Hautes Etudes en Sciences Sociales (EHESS) and the Ecole Normale Superieure (ENS). The series hosts the texts of the lectures or the monographs they inspire.

Jean Nicod Committee

Jacques Bouveresse, President
Jérôme Dokic and Elisabeth Pacherie, Secretary
François Recanati, Editor of the Series

Daniel Andler	Jean-Pierre Changeux
Stanislas Dehaene	Emmanuel Dupoux
Jean-Gabriel Ganascia	Pierre Jacob
Philippe de Rouilhan	Dan Sperber

Introduction

This book arises from an introductory course titled Learning Theory and Epistemology we have been teaching jointly in the Departments of Electrical Engineering and Philosophy at Princeton University. This low-level undergraduate course serves as an introduction to aspects of philosophy, computer science, engineering, statistics, and cognitive science. It is open to all students and has no specific prerequisites other than some analytical skills and intellectual curiosity. Although much of the material is technical, we have found that the main points are both accessible to and appreciated by a broad range of students. In each class, our students have included freshmen through seniors, with majors from the sciences, engineering, humanities, and social sciences. We acknowledge with thanks a Curriculum Development Grant for this course from the 250th Anniversary Fund for Innovation in Undergraduate Education from Princeton University and are grateful to the many students who have discussed the content of the course with us.

We are indebted to conversations with Vladimir Vapnik and to comments on earlier versions from Alvin Goldman, Rajeev Kulkarni, Daniel Osherson, Joel Predd, James Pryor, Gillian

Russell, J. D. Trout, Barry Lam, Walter Sinnott-Armstrong, Maya Gupta, and Elliott Sober.

Gilbert Harman presented an earlier version of the material in this book as the 2005 Jean Nicod Lectures in Paris.

1 The Problem of Induction

In this chapter we interpret the philosophical problem of induction as a problem about the *reliability* of inductive inferences. We begin with a traditional way of raising this problem, via comparison between induction and deduction. We argue that this way of raising the problem can be misleading. We explain why deductive logic is not a theory of inference. We describe a proposal to assess inductive methods by trying to bring them into "reflective equilibrium" with particular opinions. We explain how that proposal fits with a kind of "general foundationalism" in epistemology. We then note a worry that, although the proposal may fit ordinary practice, there are reasons to think that the results of following it are at least sometimes fragile and unreliable. This returns us to our theme, namely, our interest in assessing the reliability of inductive methods. We mention ways in which this interest might be added to reflective equilibrium approaches, especially those that seek a "wide" reflective equilibrium. We end the chapter with the proposal to look to statistical learning theory to provide the basis for discussing the reliability of inferences.

1.1   The Problem

What is the problem of induction? A version of the problem is
sometimes motivated via a comparison between rules of induction and rules of deduction: valid deductive rules are necessarily
truth preserving, whereas inductive rules are not.

For example, here is a valid deductive rule:

(D)   From a premise of the form "All *F* are *G*," the
       corresponding conclusion follows of the form, "The next
       F will be *G*."

The rule (D) is illustrated in the following argument:

(DA)   All apples have seeds.
          So, the next apple will have seeds.

This argument is valid in the sense that there is no possible way
in which its premise can be true without the corresponding conclusion also being true.

A possible inductive rule might go something like this:

(I)   From considerations of the form, "Many *F* have been
       found to be *G*" and "Until now, no *F* have been found not
       to be *G*," the corresponding conclusion can be inferred of
       the form, "The next *F* will be *G*."

The rule (I) might be illustrated in the following "inductive
argument":

(IA)   Many apples have been found to have seeds.
          Until now, no apples have been found not to have seeds.
          So, the next apple will have seeds.

The "argument" (IA) is not valid in the way that the deductive
argument (DA) is valid. The "premises" of the inductive "argu-

ment" (IA) could be true even though its "conclusion" is not true: it is possible that all apples examined until now have had seeds and yet the next apple will not have seeds. That same possibility does not impugn the validity of the deductive rule (D), because if the next apple does not have seeds that means that the first premise of the deductive argument (DA) is false—it won't be true that all apples have seeds. It is not possible that all apples have seeds and the next apple does not have seeds. But it is possible that all apples examined until now have had seeds and yet the next apple does not have seeds.

Valid deduction therefore has a kind of perfect *conditional reliability* that induction lacks. In light of this consideration, one problem of induction is the problem of saying in what way inductive rules are reliable.

This issue about the reliability of induction is not the same as the issue of whether it is possible to produce a noncircular justification of induction. That issue arises when one considers how to justify one or another inductive rule. It may seem that the only possible justification would go something like this.

Induction has been pretty reliable in the past.

So, induction will be pretty reliable in the future.

Any such justification would seem to be circular because it uses an inductive principle to justify an inductive principle. (Perhaps we can justify one inductive principle in terms of another, but it would seem that ultimately there will be an inductive principle for which we can supply no noncircular justification.)

In any event, our problem of induction is not the issue of noncircular justification. To a first approximation, our problem is this: A deductive rule like (D) is perfectly reliable in the sense that, necessarily, it never leads from true premises to a false conclusion. An inductive rule like (I) is not perfectly reliable in that sense. There are instances of (I) with true "premises" but false "conclusions." Our problem of induction, then, is to explain what sort of reliability an inductive rule might have and to specify inductive rules that have that sort of reliability.

It might be suggested that we can measure the reliability of a rule like (I) by the percentage of instances with true premises that have true conclusions. But the rule has infinitely many instances with true premises, infinitely many of which have false conclusions and infinitely many of which have true conclusions. Given infinitely many cases of each sort, the percentage of instances with true conclusions is not clearly defined. We might consider only inductive arguments of the form that people have actually made or will make, presumably a finite number, in which case reliability might be measured as the percentage of actual inferences of this sort with true premises that also have true conclusions. But this would not provide a measure of the reliability of those inductive rules that people have not and never will use, and which might be more or less reliable than rules people actually use. So, we might consider the percentage of inferences of the relevant form with true premises that *would* also have true conclusions if people *were* to make inferences of that form. However, it isn't clear how to evaluate such a counterfactual criterion. A better idea is to consider the *statistical probability* that inferences of that form with true premises would also have true conclusions.

But before we discuss this appeal to statistical probability we need to discuss an oversimplification in the somewhat standard way in which we have stated this problem of induction.

1.2   Inference and Implication

Following tradition, we have been writing as if there were two kinds of reasoning, deductive and inductive, with two kinds of arguments, deductive and inductive. That traditional idea is confused, and correcting the confusion complicates the way the issue of inductive reliability is to be formulated.

In the traditional view, reasoning can be modeled by a formal proof or argument or argument sketch. One starts by accepting certain premises, and then accepts intermediate conclusions that follow from the premises or earlier intermediate conclusions in accordance with certain rules of inference. One ends by accepting new conclusions that one has inferred directly or indirectly from the original premises.

In the traditional view, a deductive logic is a theory of reasoning. Deductive logic is concerned with deductive rules of inference like (D). Since we have a good deductive logic, it has been suggested that we need an inductive logic that specifies inductive rules of inference like (I).

The trouble is that this traditional picture of the relation between induction and deduction conflates two quite different things, namely, a theory of reasoning and a theory of what follows from what.

An obvious difficulty with the traditional picture is its implication that reasoning is always a matter of inferring new things from what one starts out believing. On the contrary, reasoning often involves abandoning things one starts out believing. For example, one discovers an inconsistency in one's beliefs and so reasons about which belief to give up. Or one starts by accepting a particular datum that one later rejects as an "outlier." More generally, one regularly modifies previous opinions in light of new information.

A related problem with the traditional picture is its treatment of deductive principles as rules of inference. In fact, they are not rules of inference, but rules about what follows from what. Consider rule (R):

(R)   From premises of the form "All *F* are *G*" and "*a* is *F*" the corresponding conclusion of the form "*a* is *G*" follows.

(R) says that a certain conclusion follows from certain premises. It is not a rule of inference. It does not say, for example, that if one believes "All *F* are *G*" and also believes "*a* is *F*" one may or must infer "*a* is *G*." That putative rule of inference is not generally correct, whereas the rule about what follows from what holds necessarily and universally.

The alleged rule of inference is not generally correct because, for example, one might already believe "*a* is not *G*" or have good reason to believe it. In that case, it is not generally true that one may or must also infer and come to believe "*a* is *G*." Perhaps one should instead stop believing "All *F* are *G*" or "*a* is *F*." Perhaps one should put all one's energy into trying to figure out the best response to this problem, which may involve gathering more data. Or perhaps one should go have lunch and think about how to resolve this problem later.

From inconsistent beliefs, everything follows. But it is not the case that from inconsistent beliefs one can infer everything.

Deductive logic is a theory of what follows from what, not a theory of reasoning. It is a theory of deductive consequence. Deductive rules like (R) are absolutely universal rules, not default rules; they apply to any subject matter at all, and are not specifically principles about a certain process or activity. Principles of reasoning are specifically principles about a particular process, namely a process of reasoning. If there is a principle of reasoning that corresponds to (R), it holds only as a default principle, that is, "other things being equal."

Deductive arguments have premises and conclusions. Reasoning does not in the same way have premises and conclusions. If we want to say that the "premises" of inductive reasoning are the beliefs from which we reason, it is important to note that some of those "beliefs" may be given up in the course of our reasoning. A logical proof or "argument" is an abstract structure of propositions;[1] reasoning, on the other hand, is a process or activity.

Sometimes in reasoning, we do construct a more or less formal proof or argument. But we do not normally construct the argument by first thinking of the premises, then the intermediate steps, and finally the conclusion. We do not generally construct the argument from premises to conclusion. Often we work backward from the desired conclusion. Or we start in the middle and work forward toward the conclusion of the argument and backward toward the premises.

Sometimes we reason to the best explanation of some data, where the explanation consists in an explanatory argument. In such a case, the *conclusion* of the explanatory argument represents the "premises" of our reasoning, the data to be explained, and the "conclusion" of our reasoning is an explanatory *premise* of the argument.

It is a category mistake to treat deduction and induction as belonging to the same category. Deductive arguments are

---

1. Of course, there are other senses of the word *argument* for example to refer to a dispute among two or more people.

abstract structures of propositions, whereas inductive reasoning is a process of change in view. There are deductive arguments, but it is a category mistake to speak of deductive reasoning except in the sense of reasoning *about* deductions. There is inductive reasoning, but it is a category mistake to speak of inductive arguments. There is deductive logic, but it is a category mistake to speak of inductive logic.

One might object that there is a perfectly standard terminology used by some logicians according to which certain deductive rules are called "rules of inference." How could we object to this terminology? Our answer is that this is like saying that there is a perfectly standard terminology used by some gamblers according to which the so-called gambler's fallacy is a legitimate principle about probability: "That's just how those gamblers use the term *probable*!" The gambler's fallacy is a real fallacy, not just a terminological difference. It can have terrible results. In the same way, to call deductive rules "rules of inference" is a real fallacy, not just a terminological matter. It lies behind attempts to develop relevance logics and inductive logics that are thought better at capturing ordinary reasoning than classical deductive logic, as if deductive logic offers a partial theory of ordinary reasoning. It makes logic courses difficult for students who do not see how the deductive rules are rules of inference in any ordinary sense. It is just wrong for philosophers and logicians carelessly to continue to use this "terminology," given the disastrous effects it has had and continues to have on education and logical research.

We are not arguing that there is *no* relation between deductive logic and reasoning. Our limited point here is that deductive rules are rules about what follows from what, not rules about what can be inferred from what. Maybe, as has often been suggested, it is an important principle of reasoning that, roughly speaking, one should avoid believing inconsistent things, where logic provides an account of one sort of consistency. But whether or not there is such a principle and how to make it more precise and accurate is an interesting question that is not to be settled within deductive logic.

Similar remarks apply to the thought that principles of inductive reasoning have to do with rational or subjective degrees of belief, where consistency then includes not violating the axioms of the probability calculus. One sort of theory of probability is an abstract mathematical subject. How it is to be applied to reasoning is not part of the mathematics. The same point holds for decision theories that appeal to utilities as well as probabilities. These theories offer extended accounts of consistency or "coherence" of belief but leave open in what way such consistency or coherence is relevant to reasoning.

Various theories of belief revision are sometimes described as logics, not just because there is a use of the term "logic" to refer to methodology but because these theories of belief revision have certain formal aspects. As will become clear in what follows, we certainly have no objection to the attempt to provide formal or mathematical theories or models of reasoning of this sort. We very much want to develop models that are, on the one hand, psychologically plausible or implementable in a machine and are, on the other hand, such that it is possible to know something useful about their reliability.

To repeat the point of this section: it is a mistake to describe the problem of inductive reliability by comparison with deductive reliability. Deductive rules are rules about what follows from what; they are not rules about what can be inferred from what.

1.3 Reflective Equilibrium

Induction is a kind of reasoned change in view in which the relevant change can include subtraction as well as addition. Can anything specific be said about how people actually reason? And can anything specific be said about the reliability of their reasoning?

One obvious point is that actual reasoning tends to be "conservative" in the sense that the number of new beliefs and methods added and old beliefs and methods given up in any given instance of reasoned change in view will be quite small in comparison with the number of beliefs and methods that stay the same. The default is not to change.

At least two things can lead us to make reasoned changes in our beliefs—changes that are the result of reasoning. First, we may want to answer a question on which we currently have no opinion; reasoning from our present beliefs can then lead us to add one or more new beliefs. Second, we may find that some of our beliefs are inconsistent with or in tension with others; reasoning from our presently conflicting beliefs can then lead us to abandon some of those beliefs.

In making changes of either sort, we try to pursue positive coherence and to avoid incoherence. That is, given an interest in adding beliefs that would answer a particular question, we favor additions that positively cohere with things we already accept because, for example, the additions are implied by things we already accept, or because the addition helps to explain things we already accept. Furthermore, we try to avoid incoherence in our beliefs due to contradictions or other sorts of conflict.

Thagard (1989, 2000) has developed a "constraint satisfaction" model of coherence based reasoning using artificial neural networks, a model which has proved fruitful in research in human decision making (Holyoak and Simon 1999; Simon et al. 2001; Simon and Holyoak 2002; Read, Snow, and Simon 2003; Simon 2004). We will say more about this model below.

The coherence-based conception of reasoning plays a role in what Goodman (1953) says about justification. He is concerned with a methodological issue: How can one evaluate one's own opinions and possibly improve them? Goodman says one can test particular conclusions by seeing how they fit with general principles one accepts, and one can test general principles by considering how they fit with particular conclusions one accepts. If one's general principles conflict with one's particular judgments, one should adjust principles and particular judgments until they cohere with each other. One is then justified in accepting the resulting principles and judgments at least for the moment. Goodman sees no other way to assess one's particular judgments and general principles from within.

John Rawls (1971) refers approvingly to Goodman's discussion and says that the method of justification we have involves modifying general principles and particular judgments to better accord with each other with the aim of arriving at what he calls a "reflective equilibrium," in which general principles fit "considered" judgments about cases and judgments about cases fit the general principles.

Although Karl Popper (1934, 1979) idiosyncratically denies beliefs are ever "justified" or even that there are inductive "reasons" for belief, he too advocates a similar methodology. He advocates adopting a critical view toward our current theories, trying to find evidence that tells against them. But one should abandon a theory that has worked well only when one has found a better theory that can explain all or most of what the prior theory explained and that better survives criticism.

The reflective equilibrium method is conservative in the sense that it assumes that each of our present "considered" beliefs and methods has a kind of initial default justification; our continuing to accept such a belief or method is justified in the absence of some special challenge to it from our other "considered" beliefs and methods. In this view, all of one's current "considered" beliefs and methods represent default foundations for justification, where foundations are understood to be the starting points for justification, on a methodological interpretation of justification.

In the reflective equilibrium view of this sort of justification, the foundations are quite *general*. In contrast, what we might call *special foundations* theories are methodological theories that suppose that the default starting points for this sort of justification are more restricted. In the strictest special foundations theories (e.g., Descartes 1641), the foundations are limited to what is completely obvious and indubitable at the present time. Such strict foundations theories give rise to various traditional epistemological problems—the problem of justifying beliefs based on the testimony of others, the problem of justifying belief in other minds, the problem of justifying belief in the existence of objects in the external world, the problem of justifying beliefs about the future based on past evidence, and the problem of justifying reliance on memory.

In this sort of foundations theory of justification, the extent to which one's beliefs and methods are justified depends on how narrow the foundations are. Very narrow foundations imply that very little is justified and general skepticism results; one must abandon almost everything one believes. Such an unwelcome result can be avoided by expanding the foundations, for example, to allow that perceptual beliefs about the environment are foundational. In such an expanded foundationalism, there is no longer the same sort of epistemological problem about the external world. A certain type of inductive reasoning might be treated as a foundational method, in which case there is no longer an epistemological problem of induction. Similar proposals have been made about our ordinary reliance on memory and testimony. For example, Burge (1993) and Foley (1994) might be interpreted as taking reliance on testimony to be a foundational method, a suggestion that gets rid of the otherwise intractable methodological problem of justifying reliance on testimony.

As foundations are widened, foundations theories tend more and more to resemble conservative general foundation theories, which treat all of one's considered beliefs and methods as foundational and thus avoid the traditional methodological problems. Furthermore, the very process of widening foundations in this way seems to be based on an implicit acceptance of the reflective equilibrium idea. The process occurs because the original idea of strict foundations conflicts with the particular nonskeptical judgments people find themselves committed to in ordinary life.

1.4   Worries about Reflective Equilibrium

Suppose certain inductive methods survive as we adjust our views and methods in such a way as to attain reflective equilibrium. Why should we think that this shows those methods are particularly reliable?

Goodman and Rawls say that the sort of adjustment of general principle to particular judgment is exactly how we in fact go about testing and justifying our views. But why should we assume that our ordinary methods of justification are reliable? Stich and Nisbett (1980) observe in discussing this exact issue that there is considerable evidence that our ordinary reasoning practices are affected by "heuristics and biases" (Tversky and Kahneman 1974), which can and often do produce clearly unreliable results.

To be sure, the fact that we can tell that these results are unreliable might indicate only that people are ordinarily not in reflective equilibrium. A similar response might be made to Stich and Nisbett's suggestion that the gambler's fallacy might well survive ordinary reflective equilibrium. The gambler's fallacy is a fallacy only when it is inconsistent with other beliefs of the gambler having to do with probabilistic independence of certain events. Goodman and Rawls might deny that beliefs could be in reflective equilibrium if they were inconsistent in a way that reflection could reveal.

Stich and Nisbett argue that in determining which methods are reasonable to use, we cannot rely on ordinary opinion even if it is in reflective equilibrium. They say we need instead to take expert opinion into account. But how do we determine who the experts are? And why should we trust them anyway?

A possibly more serious worry about ordinary reflective equilibrium is that it appears to exhibit an unwelcome fragility that undermines its claim to reliability.

We mentioned earlier that Thagard (1989, 2000) develops models of the method of reflective equilibrium using connectionist constraint satisfaction. These models exhibit this worrisome fragility. The models contain networks of nodes representing particular propositions. A node receives positive excitation to the extent that it is believed and negative excitation to the extent that it is disbelieved. There are two sorts of links among nodes, positive and negative. Positive links connect nodes with others that they explain or imply or stand in some sort of evidential relation to, so that as one of the nodes becomes more excited, the node's excitation increases the excitation of the other nodes, and as one such node becomes less excited or receives negative excitation, that decreases the excitation of the other nodes.

Negative links connect nodes that conflict with each other so that as one such node receives more excitation, the others receive less and vice versa. Excitation, positive and negative, cycles round and round the network until it eventually settles into a relatively steady state. Nodes in the steady state that have a positive excitation above a certain threshold represent beliefs, and nodes in the final state that have a negative excitation beyond a certain threshold represent things that are disbelieved. Nodes in the final state with intermediate excitation values represent things that are neither believed nor disbelieved. The resulting state of the network represents a system of beliefs in some sort of equilibrium.

It has often been noted that a connectionist network provides a possible model of certain sorts of Gestalt perception (Feldman 1981). Consider a Necker cube (figure 1.1). A given vertex might be perceived either as part of the near surface or as part of the back surface. This aspect of the perception of a Necker cube can be modeled in a connectionist network, using nodes to represent vertices, and setting up positive links among the vertices connected by horizontal or vertical lines and negative links between vertices connected by diagonal lines, where the degree of

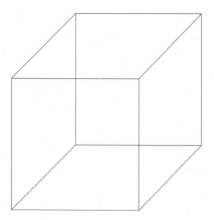

Figure 1.1
A Necker cube.

excitation of a vertex is used to represent how near it seems to the perceiver. As excitation on a given vertex increases, that increases the excitation on the three other vertices of that face and drives down the excitation of the vertices on the other face. The result is that one tends to see the figure with one or the other face in front and the other in back. One tends not to see the figure as some sort of mixture or as indeterminate as to which face is in front.

Thagard (1989) has used his constraint-satisfaction connectionist network to model the reasoning of jurors trying to assess the guilt of someone in a trial. The model makes certain predictions. For example, a juror might begin with a view about the reliability of a certain sort of eye-witness identification, a view about whether posting a message on a computer bulletin board is more like writing something in a newspaper or more like saying something in a telephone conversation, and so forth. Suppose the case being decided depends in part on an assessment of such matters. Then Thagard's model predicts that a juror's general confidence in this type of eye-witness identification should increase if the juror judges that in this case the testimony was correct and should decrease if the juror judges that in this case the testimony was not correct; the model predicts a similar effect on the juror's judgment about what posting on a computer network is more similar to, and so forth. The model also predicts that, because of these effects, the juror's resulting reflective equilibrium will lead to the juror's being quite confident in the verdict he or she reaches.

Experiments involving simulated trials have confirmed this prediction of Thagard's model (Simon 2004). In these experiments, subjects are first asked their opinions about certain principles of evidence about various sorts of eyewitness identifications, resemblances, and so on. Then they are given material about difficult cases involving such considerations to think about. Finally, the subjects' final verdicts and their confidence in their verdicts and in the various principles of evidence are recorded.

One result is that, as predicted, although subjects may divide in their judgments of guilt at the end, with some saying the defendant is guilty and others denying this, subjects are very confident in their judgments and in the considerations that support them. Furthermore, also as predicted, there are changes in subjects' judgments about the value of that sort of eye-witness identification, about whether posting on a computer bulletin board is more like writing in a newspaper or having a private conversation, and so forth.

The model implies that judgments in these hard cases are sometimes fragile and unreliable. When there is conflicting evidence, there is considerable tension among relevant considerations, just as there is a certain sort of tension among the nodes representing vertices in the Necker cube problem. If some nodes acquire even slightly increased or decreased excitation, the relevant inhibitory and excitatory connections can lead to changes in the excitation of other nodes in a kind of chain reaction or snowballing of considerations leading to a clear verdict, one way or the other, depending on the initial slight push, just as happens in one's perception of a Necker cube.

After the Gestalt shift has occurred, however, the case seems quite clear to the juror because the juror's confidence has shifted in response to the positive and negative connections between nodes.

One upshot of this is that the slight errors in a trial that look like "harmless errors" can have profound effects that cannot be corrected later by telling jurors to ignore something. By then the "ignored" evidence may have affected the excitation of various other items in such a way that the damage cannot be undone. Similarly, the fact that the prosecution goes first may make a difference by affecting how later material is evaluated.

This fragility of reflective equilibrium casts doubt on using the method of reflective equilibrium to arrive at reliable opinions.

This sort of problem has been noted in discussions of Rawls's claim that justification of views about justice consists in getting one's judgments into reflective equilibrium. It is sometimes suggested that the problem might be met by trying to find a "wide" rather than a "narrow" reflective equilibrium, where that involves not only seeing how one's current views fit together but also considering various other views and the arguments that might be given for them, and trying to try to avoid the sorts of effects that arise from the order in which one gets evidence or thinks about an issue (Daniels 1979). One needs to consider how things would have appeared if one had gotten evidence and thought about issues in a different order, for example. In this way one tries to find a *robust* reflective equilibrium, one that is not sensitive to small changes in one's starting point or the order in which one considers various considerations.

Experimenters have shown that if subjects acting as jurors are instructed to try for this sort of wide robust reflective equilibrium, they are less subject to the sorts of effects that occur when they are not (Simon 2004).

Does this mean that inductive methods endorsed by wide robust reflective equilibrium are reliable? Maybe, but why should we think so? Once we come to doubt the reliability of methods endorsed by narrow reflective equilibrium, why should we believe in the reliability of inductive methods accepted in wide robust reflective equilibrium? At this point, it does not seem adequate to be content to say that this is simply how we justify things and leave it at that.

1.5   Reliability

Thagard (1988, chapter 7) argues for an extension of the method of wide robust reflective equilibrium that also takes into account what one takes to be the best examples of reasoning in the history of science as well as one's understanding of the goals of inquiry. These goals might well include finding reliable inductive methods.

But how do we tell which methods good reasoners use and how can we assess the reliability of these methods as compared with other, possibly better, methods?

Given a number of possible reasoning methods, one way to proceed is to consider a variety of reasoning problems that actually arise in practice, to find out what is recommended in each case by each of the methods, and to see which method ends up giving better results. Bishop and Trout (2005, pp. 13–14) mention such examples as predicting the success of medical interventions, predicting criminal recidivism, predicting tomorrow's weather, predicting academic performance, predicting loan and credit risk, and predicting the quality of a French wine vintage. For some examples of this sort it has been possible to obtain information about the comparative reliability of expert predictions as compared with each other and with certain simple linear models based on only some of the data available to the experts. As Bishop and Trout explain, in many areas, certain simple linear models provide more reliable predictions than experts.

So, one way to proceed is to study empirically how well various inductive methods do in real life. Such a study might be part of one kind of wide reflective equilibrium. But it is also useful to approach the question of inductive reliability in a more theoretical way through statistical learning theory.

Statistical learning theory has an empirical aspect, a mathematical aspect, and a philosophical or conceptual aspect. Its empirical aspect is reflected in its application to the development of useful techniques for "machine learning." Its philosophical or conceptual aspect consists in the elaboration of certain ways of conceiving of inductive inference—certain inferential or learning paradigms. Its mathematical aspect consists in various results concerning those paradigms. The interplay between these aspects connects these results to practice and to a variety of assumptions or presuppositions that one might make in thinking about the reliability of inductive methods.

Of course, what can be proved depends on the assumptions made. We do not suggest that there is a deductive or mathematical justification of induction. Our point is that certain conceptual developments in statistical learning theory, which have proved to be practically useful in developing learning algorithms, are also philosophically interesting and psychologically suggestive.

1.6 A Look Ahead

To take a problem studied extensively in statistical learning theory, suppose we want a method for reaching conclusions about the next F on the basis of observing prior Fs. We want the results of the method to be correct, or correct most of the time. We are interested in finding a usable method that does as well as possible.

For example, suppose that we are interested in finding an inductive method that will use data to select a rule from a certain set C of rules for classifying new cases on the basis of their observed characteristics. Ideally, we want the method to select the best rule from C, the rule that makes the least error on new cases, the rule that minimizes expected error on new cases.

In other words, suppose that each rule in C has a certain "expected error" on new cases. We want a method for finding the rule with the least expected error, given enough data.

But what does it mean to talk about the "expected error" of a rule from C? We might identify the expected error with the (unknown) frequency of actual errors we will make using the rule. But as we mentioned earlier, we will want to consider the expected error for rules we don't use, where there is no frequency of actual errors. So perhaps we need to consider the frequency of errors we would make if we used the rule, which is perhaps to say that the expected error of a rule is the (unknown) probability of error using that rule.

But where does that probability come from? We are concerned with the actual reliability of one or another rule, which presumably cannot be identified with our degree of belief in the rule or even with any sort of epistemic probability. We suggest that claims about actual reliability presuppose a possibly unknown objective background statistical probability rather than any sort of evidential probability.

Without getting into deep philosophical issues about the nature of probability, let us say that we believe it makes sense to speak of statistical probability only in relation to a level of analysis of a system as a certain sort of "chance set-up," to use Hacking's (1965) useful terminology. It may be that a process involving a roulette wheel can be described as a chance set-up at one level of analysis, as a deterministic process at a deeper level, and as a chance set-up again, at an even deeper level. Our present point is that the relevant sort of reliability has application only with reference to a level of analysis of a situation as a chance set-up in which the relevant statistical probabilities make sense. There are important issues about the interpretation of this sort of probability that we will not discuss here, except to say that this kind of probability plays an important role in various contemporary subjects studied in engineering, computer science, and statistics, including statistical learning theory.

Earlier we said we were interested in finding an inductive method for using data to select a rule from a certain set C of rules for classifying new cases on the basis of their observed characteristics. The rules in C will be rules for estimating the classification of an item given observed characteristics. We want to find a rule from C whose expected error as measured by that background probability distribution is as low as possible.

Any conclusion about inductive reliability of the sort with which we are concerned presupposes such a background probability distribution. To seek a method that is reliable in this way is to seek a method that is reliable in relation to that probability distribution. Without the assumption of such an unknown background statistical probability distribution, it does not make sense to talk about this sort of reliability.

The next question is this. How can we use data to choose a good rule from C? One obvious idea is to select a rule from C with the least error on the data. Then we use that rule in order to classify new data. This is basically the method of enumerative induction. Our question, then, is: How good is this version of enumerative induction for choosing a rule from C?

Clearly, it depends on what rules are in the set C from which a rule is to be chosen. If all possible rules are in that set, then there will be many rules with least error on the data, and these will give completely different advice about new cases. So, enumerative induction will not favor some predictions about new cases over others.

More generally, any inductive method must have some sort of *inductive bias*. It must prefer some rules over others. It must be biased in favor of some rules and against others. If the method is the sort of enumerative induction which selects a rule from C with the least error on the data, there has to be a restriction on what rules are in C. Otherwise, we will not be able to use data in that particular way to restrict the classifications of new cases.

Notice furthermore that restricting the rules in C will sometimes allow enumerative induction to select a rule that is not completely in accord with the data. Accepting such a rule is not to accept that the data are completely correct. So, enumerative induction can involve giving up something previously accepted.[2]

Of course, restricting the rules in C runs the risk of not including the best of all possible rules, the rule with the least expected error on new cases. That is a problem with this sort of enumerative induction because there is no way to use such enumerative induction to classify new cases without restricting the rules in C.

There are other possible inductive methods for choosing rules—methods that do not just choose the rule with the least error on the data. One such method balances data-coverage against something else, such as the simplicity of a given rule. In that case, the idea is to choose a rule that has the best combination of data-coverage and this other factor as measured in one or another way. We will say a little about that idea in a moment, but now let us concentrate on what is needed for the sort of enumerative induction that simply chooses the rule in C with the least error on the data. The present point is that such simple enumerative induction cannot include all possible rules in C.

So now consider the question of how the rules in C might be restricted if enumerative induction in this sense is to be guaranteed to work, given enough evidence, no matter what the background statistical probability distribution.

The answer to this question is one of the great discoveries of statistical learning theory—the discovery of the importance of the *Vapnik-Chervonenkis* dimension, or VC dimension, of a set of rules. The VC dimension is a measure of the "richness" of the set of rules and it is inversely related to the degree of falsifi-

2. Also, if new data are obtained, the rule that enumerative induction selects can change, which is another way in which it may involve giving up something previously accepted.

ability of the set.[3] Roughly speaking, Vapnik and Chervonenkis' (1968) fundamental result is that enumerative induction in the relevant sense can be shown to work, given enough data, no matter what the background statistical probability distribution, iff the set C has finite VC dimension. We describe this result in more detail in our second chapter.

As we mentioned, enumerative induction in this sense is not the only possible inductive method. But it is a method that applies to many examples of machine learning, including perceptron learning and feed-forward neural net learning.

The other method we mentioned, in which data-coverage is balanced against something else, allows for choosing among a set of rules with infinite VC dimension. Here it can be shown that the right thing to balance against data-coverage is not simplicity conceived in any usual way, such as the number of parameters used to specify a particular member of a class of rules. We will discuss this in our third chapter.

Vapnik (1979, 1998, 2000) describes a method of inference that (e.g., in Vapnik 2000, p. 293) he calls "transduction," a method that in a certain sense infers directly from data to the classification of new cases as they come up. Under certain conditions, transduction gives considerably better results than those obtained from methods that use data to infer a rule that is then

3. More precisely, the VC dimension of a set of rules C is the maximum number of data points that can be arranged so that C "shatters" those points. C shatters N data points iff for every one of the 2^N ways of assigning values to each of those points there is a rule in C that is in accord with that assignment. Vapnik connects the role of VC dimension with Popper's (1934) discussion of the importance of falsifiability in science.

used to classify new cases (Joachims 1999; Vapnik 2000; Weston et al. 2003; Goutte et al. 2004). We will discuss this in our fourth chapter.

Our point for now is that the problem of induction as we have described it—the problem of finding reliable inductive methods—can be and is being fruitfully investigated in statistical learning theory (Vapnik 1998; Kulkarni et al. 1998; Hastie et al. 2001).

1.7 Conclusion

Let us sum up. The problem of induction as we have been understanding it is the problem about the *reliability* of inductive inference. The problem is sometimes motivated by comparing induction with deduction, a comparison that we have argued rests on confusing issues about what follows from what with issues about what can be inferred from what. Deduction has to do with what follows from what; induction has to do with what can be inferred from what.

Some have suggested that the only real problem is to try to specify how we actually perform inductive reasoning. In this view issues about reliability are to be answered by adjusting one's methods and beliefs so that they fit together in a reflective equilibrium. While there is evidence that people do reason by adjusting their opinions in the way suggested, there is also considerable evidence that the results are fragile and unreliable, and it is hard to be in reflective equilibrium if we do not believe our methods of reasoning are reliable. Furthermore, there is empirical evidence that people often reason in ways that are less reliable than very simple alternative methods. Given that reasoning often involves giving up things previously believed, it may seem unclear how even to specify the desired type of reliability.

However, it does turn out to be possible to specify methods for doing one sort of enumerative induction and to address questions about their reliability. These questions can be and have been studied empirically and also theoretically in statistical learning theory, a theory that has implications for other possible inductive methods as well.

2 Induction and VC Dimension

2.1 Pattern Recognition

The problem of inductive reliability can be seen as a problem in learning theory. It is the problem of finding reliable ways to learn from data. For example, how can one find and assess inductive *methods* for using data to arrive at reliable *rules* for classifying new cases or estimating the value of a real variable?

In thinking about this problem, two kinds of methods or rules must be carefully distinguished. Rules of classification or estimation must be carefully distinguished from inductive methods for finding such rules. Rules of classification or estimation are rules for using observed *features* of items to classify them or to estimate the values of a real variable. Inductive methods for finding such rules are methods for using *data* to select such rules of classification or estimation.

In the previous chapter we discussed a particular method, *enumerative induction*. In this chapter, we will say more about using enumerative induction to learn rules of classification and to estimate the values of real variables. In our next chapter we discuss some other methods for using data to arrive at rules of classification or estimation.

In our fourth and final chapter we will go beyond these sorts of *inductive* methods to discuss methods of *transduction* that do not (in a certain sense) first use data to arrive at rules of classification or estimation that are then used to classify new cases or estimate values of a real variable for new cases as they arise. These methods use information about what new cases have actually come up in deciding what to say about the new cases. But in this second chapter and the next third chapter we will be concerned only with inductive methods for coming up with rules of classification or estimation.

An inductive method is a principle for finding a *pattern* in the data that can then be used to classify new cases or to estimate the values of a real variable. So, the problem of finding a good inductive method is sometimes called a *pattern recognition* problem (Bongard 1970; Duda, Hart, and Stork 2001).

2.1.1 Pattern Classification

In a pattern classification problem, we seek to come up with a rule for using observable features of objects in order to classify them into one of a finite number of categories, where each feature can take several possible values, which can be represented by real numbers. In the most common case there are just two categories, so this is the case we consider here. For purposes of medical diagnosis, values of the features could represent the results of certain medical tests. For recognition of written addresses on envelopes, the relevant area of an envelope could be represented by a grid of $W \times H$ pixels, with a feature value for each pixel representing the intensity of light at the pixel, so there would be $W \times H$ different features. For face recognition from color photographs using a grid of $W \times H$ pixels, feature values could include representations of each of the RGB values of each pixel (the intensities of red, green, and blue components of the color of the pixel), so there would be $3 \times W \times H$ features.

Each observable feature can be treated as a dimension in a D-dimensional *feature space*. If there is a single feature, F, the feature space is one-dimensional, a line. A point in the feature space has a single F coordinate representing the value of that feature. If there are two features, F_1 and F_2, the feature space is the two-dimensional plane and each point has two coordinates, an F_1 coordinate and a F_2 coordinate, indicating the values of those two features. If there are three features, F_1, F_2, and F_3, a point in the three-dimensional feature space has an F_1 coordinate, representing the value of feature F_1, an F_2 coordinate, representing the value of feature F_2, and an F_3 coordinate, representing the value of feature F_3.

In the case of the $H \times W$ color pixels, there are $3 \times H \times W$ dimensions to this space. Each point in this large feature space has $3 \times H \times W$ coordinates. Each such point represents a particular possible color picture, a particular way of assigning feature values to the color pixels.

Data for learning can then be represented by labeled points in the feature space. The coordinates of each such point represent an object with the corresponding feature values. The label indicates a classification of that object, perhaps as provided by an "expert."

A possible new case to be categorized is then represented by an unlabeled point, the inductive task being to interpolate or extrapolate labelings from already labeled data points to the unlabeled point (figure 2.1).

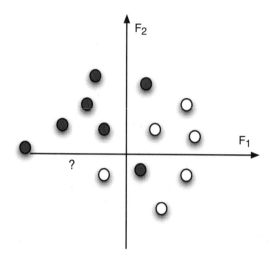

Figure 2.1
Feature space: Gray dots label points that are categorized as YESes; white dots label points that are categorized as NOs. The point at the question mark is unlabeled.

2.1.2 Estimating the Value of a Real Variable

A related problem is the problem of using data in order to estimate the value of a real variable. This problem is like a categorization problem in which the value of the real variable is the correct labeling of a point in feature space. However, there are two important differences between categorization and real variable estimation. One difference is that categorization involves applying one of a small finite number of possible categories (for example, two—YES and NO), while the possible values of a real-valued variable can be nondenumerably infinite. This gives rise to the second difference, which is that in esimation it is not useful to consider the probability of an incorrect estimate. Instead,

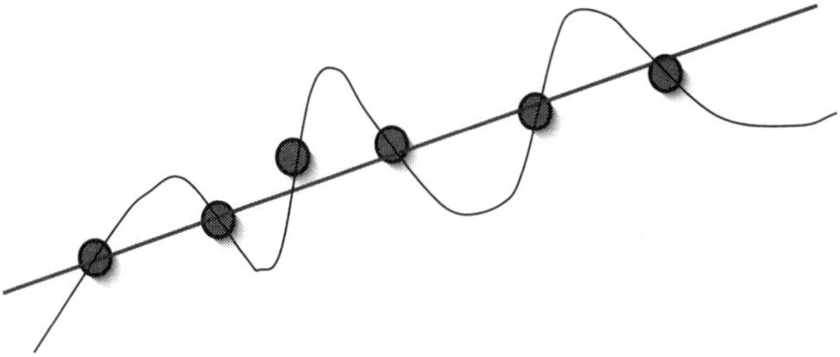

Figure 2.2
Curve fitting.

it is more appropriate to consider how close one real value is to another (rather than whether they are exactly the same).

A variable estimation problem can be considered a "curve fitting problem" if the estimated values of the variable are represented by a "curve" (or hypersurface) in $D + 1$ dimensional space. To take a very simple example (figure 2.2), assume that our estimate of the real variable y will be a function $f(x)$ of one argument x and our task is to use data to find a function that provides the best estimate of y. Each datum can be represented as a point in the plane, where the x coordinate represents the value of the argument and the y coordinate represents the value of the estimation function according to that particular datum. The task is to estimate y by fitting a curve to the data.

2.2 Background Probability Distribution

In general, in classification problems there will not be a perfect correlation between observed features and the best classifications of objects with those features. For one thing, there may be *noise* or errors in measurement in the observed features.

Furthermore, the relation between features and classification may be at best merely probabilistic even apart from issues of noise. For example, suppose the task is to recognize whether a person is currently happy, given only a picture of the expression on his or her face. It may very well be true that a person with a certain visual expression is sometimes happy and sometimes sad, so that the relation between the features revealed in that picture and the correct classification of the person as happy or sad is only probabilistic.

Similarly, estimation of a real valued variable must allow for noise in the data, as well as the possibility that the variable depends on other factors than those we use to make our estimate.

We have already suggested that questions about the reliability of inductive conclusions presuppose that there is a possibly unknown background statistical probability distribution. Discussions of the reliability of a rule of classification presuppose that there is a statistical probabilistic connection between observable features and correct classification. And discussions of the reliability of a rule of estimation of a real valued variable presuppose that there is a statistical probabilistic connection between observable features and the value of the variable given those features.

So, we assume that there is a background probability distribution P which (among other things) defines the conditional probabilities that an item is correctly classified as an A given that it has certain observed features, $P(A|F_1 \& F_2 \& F_3 \& \ldots)$. Or we assume that the background probability P defines in this way the conditional probabilities that the value of a given variable is A given the observation of features whose values are $F_1 \& F_2 \& F_3 \& \ldots$. (In many contexts, conditional probability densities are required, rather than simple conditional probabilities. See, for example, Duda, Hart, and Stork 2001.)

In other words, we assume that the data represent a random sample arising from the background probability distribution, and we assume that new cases that are encountered are also randomly produced by that distribution. We do not assume that we know what that distribution is. We do not assume it is a normal distribution or that its mean, standard deviation, and so on are known. This is a problem in "nonparametric statistics," because nothing is assumed about the parameters of the background probability distribution.

The only assumptions made about the background probability distribution are that (1) the probability of the occurrence of an item with certain features and classification is independent of the occurrence of other items, and (2) the same distribution governs the occurrence of each item. One familiar example of an assumption of probabilistic independence and identical distribution is the assumption that the probability that a tossed coin will come up heads is independent of the results of other tosses and that the probability of heads for each toss is the same. (Given a theory based on an assumption of such probabilistic independence and identical distribution, it may be possible to extend the theory by relaxing the assumptions of independence and identical distribution, but we will not consider such extensions in this book.)

The gambler's fallacy, mentioned briefly in the previous chapter, rests on a confusion about probabilistically independent events. After a tossed coin has come up heads four times in a row, the gambler's fallacy leads to the thought that the probability of heads on the next toss is considerably greater than one half "because heads is due."

This thought may rest on the following reasoning:

The coin is fair, so it should come up heads about half the time in a long enough string of tosses. In particular, it is quite probable that heads will come up between four and six times in ten tosses. Since heads has not come up in the first four tosses, it needs to come up at least four times in the next six. So the probability of getting heads on the next toss is at least 4/6.

This reasoning is mistaken. Given that the results of tosses of the coin are probabilistically independent and that the coin is fair, the probability of heads on the next toss is still 1/2. It remains true that in the long run, the frequency of heads will approach 1/2, despite the initial run of four tails. The impact of any finite number of initial results will be dwarfed by the impact of the rest of the idealized long run. The "long run" is infinitely long and thus much longer than any merely finite beginning. Any infinite series in which the frequencey of heads approaches 1/2 will continue to do so with any large finite number of tails added to its beginning.

2.3   Reliability of Rules of Classification and Estimation

2.3.1   Reliability of a Classification Rule

We have discussed the distinction between rules of classification and a method for finding those rules. We have discussed how items to be classified might be represented as points in a feature space and how data might be represented as labeled points in a feature space. We have noted that the reliability of a rule of classification depends on a possibly unknown background statistical probability distribution. And we have noted that we might be able to make only minimal assumptions about that background probability distribution, namely, the assumption of probabilistic independence and identical distribution (although as we have mentioned, this assumption can be relaxed in various ways).

We can now distinguish two questions.

1. With respect to the (unknown) background probability distribution what is a best rule of classification?

2. If the background probability distribution is unknown, under what conditions can data be used to find a best (or good enough) rule of classification?

One possible answer to the first question is that the best rule is the one that minimizes the expected frequency of error, where the expected frequency of error is determined by the probability (according to the unknown background probability distribution) that a use of the rule will lead to an error.

That answer assumes all errors are equally bad. If certain sorts of errors are worse than others, that can be taken that into account. It could happen, for example, in medical testing, where false positives might be less serious than false negatives. We might then assign different weights or costs to different sorts of errors and then treat the best rule as the one that minimizes expected cost.

The best rule is standardly called the "Bayes Rule" (see, e.g., Hastie et al. 2001, p. 21). Given the (unknown) background probability distribution, the Bayes Rule is the rule that for each set of features chooses the classification with the smallest expected cost, given that set of features. In the special case in which all errors are equally bad, the Bayes Rule is the rule that chooses, for each set of features, the classification with greatest conditional probability given that set of features, which results in the smallest probability of error. (For simplicity in what follows we will treat all errors as equally bad and take the best rule to be the rule that simply minimizes expected error.)

2.3.2   Reliability of a Rule of Real Variable Estimation

Recall that, in addition to having to allow for noise in the data, estimation of a real valued variable must also allow for the possibility that the variable in question is only probabilistically related to observable features of the data. So, given values of those observable features, there will be various possible values of the real variable, values whose probabilities (or probability densities) are determined by the unknown background probability distribution. On a particular occasion when those are the values of the observable features, the real variable will have a particular value. The amount of error on that occasion of a particular estimate of the value of the function for those values of the arguments might be measured by the absolute value of the difference between the estimate and the value of the variable on that occasion, or by the square of that difference. More generally, the expected error of an estimate with respect to given observable features is the sum of the possible amounts of error of the estimate for those arguments weighted by the probability of those errors (or an integral using probability densities rather than probabilities—we omit details). A rule of estimation of the value of the variable, given all possible observable features, has an *expected error* equal to the sum of its expected errors for various values of observable features weighted by the probability of observing those values of the features. (Again, normally this would be an integral rather than a sum.) In this way, any rule of real variable estimation has an expected error determined by the background probability function. The Bayes Rule for estimating a variable is then the best rule, that is, the rule for estimating that variable with the lowest expected error in general.

2.4   Inductive Learning

Is there an inductive method that will lead to the selection of the Bayes Rule, given enough data?

One way to proceed would be to try to use data first to discover or at least approximate the background probability distribution and then use that probability distribution to determine the Bayes rule. But as we shall see that turns out to be impractical. Indeed, there is no practical way of exactly finding the Bayes Rule that will work no matter what the background probability distribution given enough data.

Setting our sights somewhat lower, we can consider the following inductive learning question: To what extent can we use data to find a rule of classification or real variable estimation with performance that is as good as (or comparable to) the performance of the Bayes Rule?

The third chapter describes a positive answer to this last question. There is a sense in which we can use data to find a rule with performance that approaches the performance of the Bayes Rule as we get increasing amounts of data.

But in order to explain that answer, it will be useful to spend the rest of this chapter considering the performance of the method of enumerative induction that we began to discuss in chapter 1. There we gave an example of using enumerative induction to find a rule of categorization. Enumerative induction might also be used to find a rule of real variable estimation. Recall that enumerative induction is a method for using data to choose a rule from a restricted set of rules C: choose a rule from C with minimium error on the data.

The idea behind enumerative induction is, first, to use a rule's "empirical risk," its rate of error on the data as an estimate of its expected error on new cases and then, second, to choose a rule from C whose empirical error on the data is least.

It is possible that several rules from C are tied for having the same minimal error on the data. In that case, we will say that enumerative induction *endorses* all of the tied rules.

As we mentioned in the first chapter, this method is useful only if there are significant limits on the rules included in C. If all possible rules are included, then the rules that minimize error on the data will endorse all possible judgments for items with features that do not show up in the data—all possible interpolations and extrapolations to other cases.

On the other hand, as we also mentioned in chapter 1, if there are significant limits on the rules in C, then C might not contain the Bayes Rule, the rule with the least expected error. In fact, C might not contain any rule with expected error comparable to the minimal expected error of the Bayes Rule. The best rules in C might well have significantly greater expected error than the Bayes Rule.

Still, there will be a certain minimum expected error for rules in C. Then the goal of enumerative induction will be to find a rule with expected error that is near that minimum value. Or, since no method can be expected to find such a rule without a sufficient amount of data, the goal will be to find such a rule given a sufficient amount of data. Actually, even that goal is too ambitious in comparison with the goal of probably finding such a rule. That is to say, a realistic goal is that, with probability approaching 1, given more and more data, the expected error of a rule endorsed by enumerative induction at each stage will approach the minimum value of expected error for rules in C.

2.4.1 Linear Classification and Estimation Rules

Let us consider an example of enumerative induction to a classification rule. Recall that we are thinking of the observable features of objects as represented in a feature space. Let us suppose that we are interested in a very simple YES/NO classification of some sort. The features might be the results of D different medical tests. The classification of the person with those results might be either YES, has "metrocis" (an imaginary illness) or NO, does not have metrocis. The feature space has D dimensions, one for the result of each test. In this case any classification rule determines a set of points for which the classification is YES according to that rule. The remaining points are classified NO by the rule. So, instead of thinking of rules as linguistic or symbolic expressions, we can think about the corresponding sets of points in feature space (figure 2.3), perhaps certain scattered areas or volumes or hypervolumes of the space—"hypervolumes," because the dimensions of the feature space will typically be greater than three.

Linear classification rules are a very simple case which divide the feature space into two parts separated by a line or hyperplane, with YES on one side and NO on the other. If there are two medical tests with results F_1 and F_2, then one possible classification rule would classify the patient as having metrocis if $F_1 + 2F_2 > 6$ and otherwise classify the patient as not having metrocis. This is a linear classification rule in the sense that the rule distinguishes the YESes from the NOs by the straight line intersecting the F_2 axis at $(0, 3)$ and the F_1 axis at $(6, 0)$ (figure 2.4).

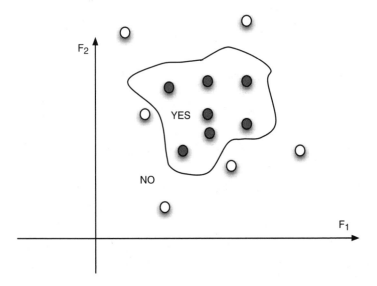

Figure 2.3
Rules as sets of points in feature space.

For any given data, it is easy to find a linear classification rule with minimum error on the data. But of course such rules are limited in what they can represent. They cannot, for example, represent an XOR rule in a two-dimensional feature space, where features can have either positive or negative values. An XOR rule classifies as a YES those and only those points for which the product of F_1 and F_2 is negative. Points classified as NO are those for which the produce is positive (because both F_1 and F_2 are positive or because both are negative). Clearly, it is not possible to separate the YES (gray) and NO (white) points in figure 2.5 using a straight line.

Of course, there are other sorts of classification rules besides linear rules. For example, there are inner circular rules as repre-

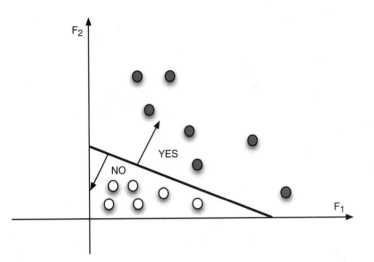

Figure 2.4
Linear classification: Metrocis.

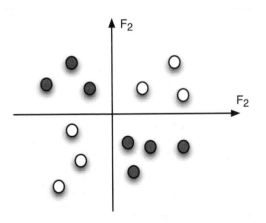

Figure 2.5
XOR representation problem for linear rules.

sented by the insides of circles or hyperspheres in the space. A rule of this sort categorizes all points inside a particular circle or hypersphere as YES and all other points as NO. There are outer circular rules, represented by the outsides of circles or hyperspheres. There are circular rules consisting in both inner and outer circular rules. There are box rules that include both inner box rules and outer box rules. There are quadrant rules that include the rule for XOR.

For any set of sets of points in feature space, there is a corresponding set of classification rules. So, there are many more classification rules than there are linguistic or symbolic representations of classification rules.

It may seem that linear categorization rules will rarely be useful.[1] But linear estimation rules are often quite useful. We noted in our first chapter a number of areas in which linear rules provide better estimates than people can, even experts—predicting the success of medical interventions, predicting criminal recidivism, predicting tomorrow's weather, predicting academic performance, predicting loan and credit risk, predicting the quality of a French wine vintage, to mention only a few (from Bishop and Trout 2005, pp. 13–14).

2.5 Conditions for Satisfactory Enumerative Induction

As we have emphasized, enumerative induction only works given a limited set C of rules. What we would like to know is what has to be true of the set C of rules if enumerative induction is to work no matter what the unknown background probability distribution.

---

1. Linear categorization rules do play an important role in support vector machines, as is explained in chapter 4, below.

In other words, what has to be true of the set C in order to guarantee that, with probability approaching 1, given more and more data, the expected error for the rules that enumerative induction endorses at each stage will approach the minimum value of expected error for rules in C?

You might wonder whether this sort of convergence isn't guaranteed by the statistical law of large numbers. That principle implies that with probability approaching 1, the empirical error of any particular rule will approach the expected error of that rule, given more and more data. But this is not the same as what is wanted. The trouble is that, given infinitely many rules, as more and more data are taken into account, the rules endorsed by enumerative induction can change infinitely often. Even if the empirical error for each rule approaches a limit, that does not imply anything about the limit of the empirical error of the varying rule endorsed by enumerative induction at each stage.

For example, C could contain a rule c_0 whose expected error is 0.1 and, in addition, an infinite series of rules $c_1, c_2, \ldots, c_n, \ldots,$ each of whose expected error is 0.5. There could be possible data so that the following happens. The empirical error of the rule c_i is 0 until the number of data points n exceeds i; thereafter, the empirical error of the rule c_i approaches 0.5. In that case, the empirical error of the varying rule endorsed by enumerative induction at each stage will be 0, but the expected error of the rules made available will always be 0.5. So, the expected error of the rules endorsed at each stage will *not* approach the minimum value of expected error for rules in C, namely 0.1.

What is needed, then, is not just that the empirical error of each rule should converge to its expected error but also that the empirical error of the varying rules endorsed by enumerative induction should approach the value of the expected error of that rule in the limit. If c_n is a rule endorsed by enumerative induction after n data points, then what is needed is that the empirical error of the rule c_n after n data points should approach the expected error of c_n in the limit. In that case, with probability approaching 1, given more and more data, the expected error of the varying rules endorsed by enumerative induction will approach in the limit the minimum value of expected error for rules in C.

This will happen if (with probability approaching 1) the empirical error of the rules in C converge *uniformly* to their expected error. Let R_c be the expected error of the rule c. Let $\hat{R}_c^n$ be the empirical error of the rule c after n data points. Let $R^n = \max_{c \in C}(|\hat{R}_c^n - R_c|)$ be the maximum value of the absolute difference between the empirical error of a rule in C and its expected error.[2] Then the empirical error of the rules in C converges uniformly to their expected error just in case R^n converges to 0 as $n \to \infty$.

What has to be true of the set of rules C for such uniform convergence? Vapnik and Chervonenkis (1968) show (in effect) that this condition is met for classification rules if and only if the set of classification rules C is not too rich, where the richness of the set is measured by what has come to be called its "VC dimension." (Results with a similar flavor hold for real variable estimation rules with suitably modified notions of dimension, but here we will discuss the result only for classification rules.)

Suppose that some set of N points in the feature space is *shattered* by rules in C in the sense that, for any possible labeling of

2. Strictly speaking, we should use the supremum (sup), or least upper bound, rather than the maximum (max) here, because with infinitely many rules in C the maximum value of the difference may not be defined.

those points, some rule in C perfectly fits the points so labeled. Then the VC dimension of the set of rules C is at least N. More specifically, the VC dimension of a set of rules C is the largest number N such that some set of N points in feature space is shattered by rules in C. If a set of rules does not have a finite VC dimension—because for any number N there is a set of N points shattered by rules in C—then the set of rules C has infinite VC dimension.

Notice that the definition of VC dimension refers to *some* set of N points being shattered, not to *all* sets of N points being shattered. Consider the set of all linear classifications of points in the plane where the YESes and NOs are separated by a straight line. The VC dimension of this set of classification rules is 3, because some set of three points in the plane can be shattered by this class of rules and no set of four points can be shattered. Three collinear points (i.e., three points on the same straight line) cannot be shattered by this class of rules, because there is no such rule that can classify the middle point as a YES and the outer points as NOs (figure 2.6). But three points that are not collinear can be shattered because, for example, any two can be separated from the third by a straight line (figure 2.7). So, the VC dimension of these linear separations is at least 3. And no four points can be shattered by this class of rules, so the VC dimension of these linear rules is exactly 3. (If any three of the

Figure 2.6
Three collinear points cannot be shattered.

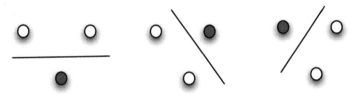

Figure 2.7
Shattering three noncollinear points in the plane.

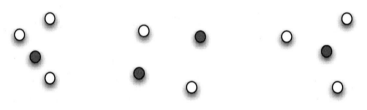

Figure 2.8
No set of four points can be shattered.

four points are collinear, the four points cannot be shattered. Otherwise, either none of the points is within the triangle defined by the other three or one of them is. Figure 2.8 indicates labelings that cannot be separated in those cases by linear rules.)

Some other examples: The VC dimension of the set of all linear separations in D-dimensional spaces is $D + 1$. The VC dimension of the set of all inner rectangles in the plane is 4. The VC dimension of the set of all unions of rectangles in the plane is infinite.

So, that is what the VC dimension comes to. Vapnik and Chervonenkis (1968) show, roughly, that enumerative induction is guaranteed to work no matter what the background probability distribution if and only if the classification rules in C have a finite VC dimension. More precisely (subject to some very mild but technical regularity conditions):

no matter what the background probability distribution,
with probability approaching 1,
as more and more data are considered,
the expected error of the rules that enumerative induction endorses will approach the minimum expected error of rules in C
if and only if
the rules in C have a finite VC dimension.

Half of this result is that, if the classification rules in C *do not*
have a finite VC dimension, then no matter how many data
points are provided, there will be probability distributions for
which enumerative induction will not select only rules with
expected error close to the minimum for rules in C. To see this,
consider what can be expected after obtaining n items of data
and let $K = 1,000,000 \times n$. Since the rules in C do not have a
finite VC dimension, there is a set of K points in the feature
space that is shattered by rules in C. Consider some probability
distribution that assigns probability $1/K$ to each member of
some such set of K points shattered by rules in C. Any subset of
those points will of course also be shattered by those rules.

So, if C does not have a finite VC dimension, then for any n
items of data, there are probability distributions that guarantee
that there are rules in C fitting whatever data are obtained but
giving all possible verdicts on all other points that might come
up, where the probability that one of these other points comes
up in any given case is very close to 1. (The probability that
one of the data points comes up again in any given case is
$1/1,000,000$.)

This is true no matter how large n is. So it is not true that, with
probability approaching 1, the expected error of the rules that
enumerative induction leads to will approach the minimum

expected error of rules in C *no matter what the background probability distribution.*

The other half of Vapnik and Chervonenkis' (1968) result is that if the rules in C *do* have a finite VC dimension, then, with probability approaching 1, the expected error of the rules endorsed by enumerative induction will approach the minimum expected error of rules in C no matter what the background probability distribution. If the rules in C have VC dimension V, there is a function $m(V, \epsilon, \delta)$ that indicates the maximum amount of data needed (no matter what the unknown background probability distribution) to ensure that the probability is less than δ that enumerative induction will endorse a hypothesis with an expected error rate that exceeds the minimum expected error rate for rules in C by more than ϵ.

Where there is such a function $m(V, \epsilon, \delta)$ there is "probably approximately correct" learning, or PAC learning (terminology due to Valiant 1984). Here a smaller ϵ indicates a better approximation to the minimum expected error for rules in C and a smaller δ indicates a higher probability that the rules endorsed will be within the desired approximation to that minimum expected error.

2.6 Popper

Vapnik (2000) sees an interesting relation between the role of VC dimension in this result and the emphasis on falsifiability in Karl Popper's writings in the philosophy of science. Popper (1934) famously argues that the difference between scientific hypotheses and metaphysical hypotheses is that scientific hypotheses are "falsifiable" in a way that metaphysical hypotheses are not. To say that a certain hypothesis is falsifiable is to say that there is possible evidence that would be inconsistent with the hypothesis.

According to Popper, evidence cannot establish a scientific hypothesis, it can only "falsify" it. A scientific hypothesis is therefore a falsifiable *conjecture*. A useful scientific hypothesis is a falsifiable hypothesis that has withstood empirical testing.

Recall that enumerative induction requires a choice of a set of rules C. That choice involves a "conjecture" that the relevant rules are the rules in C. If this conjecture is to count as scientific rather than metaphysical, according to Popper, the class of rules C must be appropriately "falsifiable."

Many discussions of Popper treat his notion of falsifiability as an all-or-nothing matter, not a matter of degree. But in fact Popper does allow for degrees of difficulty of falsifiability (2002, sections 31–40). For example, he asserts that a linear hypothesis is more falsifiable—easier to falsify—than a quadratic hypothesis. This fits with VC theory, because the collection of linear classification rules has a lower VC dimension than the collection of quadratic classification rules.

However Corfield, Schölkopf, and Vapnik (2005) observe that Popper's measure of degree of difficulty of falsifiability of a class of hypotheses does not correspond to VC dimension. Where the VC dimension of a class C of hypotheses is the largest number N such that *some* set of N points is shattered by rules in C, what we might call the "Popper dimension" of the difficulty of falsifiability of a class is the largest number N such that *every* set of N points is shattered by rules in C. This difference between *some* and *every* is important, and VC dimension turns out to be the key notion rather than Popper dimension.

Popper also assumes that the falsifiability of a class of hypotheses is a function of the number of parameters used to pick out instances of the class. This turns out not to be correct either for Popper dimension or for VC dimension, as discussed in the next chapter.

This suggests that Popper's theory of falsifiability would be improved by adopting VC dimension as the relevant measure in place of his own measure.

2.7   Summary

In this chapter we have continued our treatment of the problem of induction as a problem in statistical learning theory. We have distinguished inductive classification from inductive real variable estimation. The inductive classification problem is that of assessing inductive methods for using data to arrive at a reliable rule for classifying new cases on the basis of certain values of features of those new cases. We introduced the notion of a D-dimensional feature space, each point in the feature space representing a certain set of feature values. We assumed an unknown probability distribution that is responsible for our encounter with objects and for the correlations between feature values of objects and their correct classifications. The probability distribution determines the best rule of classification, namely the Bayes Rule that minimizes expected error.

For the special case of a YES/NO classification, we can identify a classification rule with a set of points in feature space, perhaps certain scattered areas or hypervolumes. For example, linear rules divide the space into two regions separated by a line or plane or hyperplane.

The real variable estimation problem is that of assessing inductive methods for using data about the value of a real variable given certain observed features to arrive at a reliable estimate of the value of the real variable.

Enumerative induction endorses that rule or those rules from a certain set C of rules that minimize error on the data. If enumerative induction is to be useful at all, there have to be significant limits on the rules included in C. So C may fail to contain any rule with expected error comparable to the Bayes Rule. So, we cannot expect enumerative induction to endorse a rule with expected error close to the Bayes Rule. At best it will endorse a rule with expected error close to the minimum for rules in C. And, in fact, we have to settle for its probably endorsing a rule close to the minimum for rules in C.

Vapnik and Chervonenkis (1968) show that for inductive classification, no matter what the background probability distribution, with probability approaching 1, as more and more data are considered, the expected error of the rules that enumerative induction endorses will approach the minimum expected error of rules in C, *if and only if* the rules in C have a finite VC dimension. (A similar result holds for inductive real variable estimation.)

VC dimension is explained in terms of shattering. Rules in C shatter a set of N data points if and only if for every possible labeling of the N points with YESes and NOs, there is a rule in C that perfectly fits that labeling.

In other words, there is no way to label those N points in a way that would falsify the claim that the rules in C are perfectly adequate. This points to a possible relationship between the role of VC dimension in learning by enumerative induction and the role of falsifiability in Karl Popper's methodology, a relationship to be discussed further in the next chapter.

3 Induction and "Simplicity"

3.1 Introduction

We are concerned with the reliability of inductive methods. So far we have discussed versions of enumerative induction. In this chapter, we compare enumerative induction with methods that take into account some ordering of hypotheses, perhaps by simplicity. We compare different methods for balancing data-coverage against an ordering of hypotheses in terms of simplicity or some simplicity substitute. Then we consider how these ideas from statistical learning theory might shed light on some philosophical issues. In particular, we distinguish two ways to respond to Goodman's (1953) "new riddle of induction," corresponding to these two kinds of inductive methods. We discuss some of Karl Popper's ideas about scientific method, trying to distinguish what is right and what is wrong about these ideas. Finally we consider how an appeal to simplicity or some similar ordering might provide a principled way to prefer one hypothesis over another skeptical hypothesis that is empirically equivalent with it.

3.2   Empirical Error Minimization

In chapter 2 we described an important result (Vapnik and Chervonenkis 1968) about enumerative induction. In statistical learning theory, enumerative induction is called "empirical risk minimization." In a context in which all errors are equally bad, its only criterion for choosing a rule from C is that the rule should be one of the rules in C with the least empirical error on the data. Vapnik and Chervonenkis show that the method of empirical risk minimization, when used to select rules of classification, has the following property. If, and only if, the VC dimension of C is finite, then no matter what the background probability distribution, as more and more data are obtained, with probability approaching 1, enumerative induction leads to the acceptance of rules whose expected error approaches the minimum expected error for rules in C.[1]

Moreover, when C has finite VC dimension V we can specify a function, $m(V, \epsilon, \delta)$, which indicates an upper bound to the amount of data needed to guarantee a certain probability $(1 - \delta)$ of endorsing rules with an expected error that approximates that minimum by coming within ϵ of the minimum.

Although this is a very nice result, it is also worrisome, because if C has a finite VC dimension, the best rules in C can have an expected error that is much greater than the best possible rule, the Bayes Rule. For example, if C contains only one rule that is always wrong, the best rule in C has an error rate of 1

---

1. Some very mild measurability conditions are required. And, as we mentioned, a similar result holds for enumerative induction used to select rules to estimae the value of a real variable. For the moment, we concentrate on induction to rules of classification.

even if the Bayes Rule has an error rate of 0. Even if C contains many rules and has a large VC dimension, the best rule in C may have an error rate close to .5, which is no better than random guessing, even though the Bayes Rule might have an error rate close to 0.

Recall our discussion of linear classification rules, which separate YESes and NOs in a D-dimensional feature space with a line, a plane, or a hyperplane. These rules have a VC dimension equal to $D + 1$, which is finite as long as the feature space has finite dimension, which it normally does. But linear rules are by themselves quite limited. Recall, for example, that an XOR classification rule cannot be adequately represented by a classification using a linear separation of YESes and NOs. Indeed, the best linear rule for that classification can have a very high expected error.

To be sure, we can use a class of rules C with many more rules, in addition to or instead of linear rules; we can do so as long as the VC dimension of C is finite. But no matter how high the VC dimension of C, if it is finite there is no guarantee that the expected error of the best rules in C will be close to the expected error of the Bayes Rule.

3.3 Universal Consistency

In order to guarantee that the expected error of the best classification rules in C will be close to the expected error of the best rule of all, the Bayes Rule, it is necessary that C should have infinite VC dimension. But then the nice result about enumerative induction is not forthcoming. We will not be able to specify a function $m(\infty, \delta, \epsilon)$ that would provide an upper bound to the amount of data needed to guarantee a certain probability $(1 - \delta)$

of endorsing rules whose expected error is within ϵ of the minimum expected error for rules in C, which in this case will be the error rate of the Bayes Rule.

On the other hand, there are other inductive methods for finding categorization rules that do not have the sort of guarantee of uniform convergence provided by the Vapnik-Chervonenkis result but do have a different desirable property. In particular, it can be shown that certain methods are *universally consistent*. A universally consistent method is one that, for any background probability distribution, with probability approaching 1, as more and more data are obtained, the expected error of rules endorsed by the method approaches in the limit the expected error of the best rule, the Bayes Rule.

Universal consistency does not imply uniform convergence. There may be no bound on the amount of data needed in order to ensure that (with probability approaching 1) the expected error of the rules endorsed by the method will be within ϵ of the expected error of the Bayes Rule. Nevertheless, universal consistency is clearly a desirable characteristic of a method. It does provide a convergence result, because the error rate of the rule endorsed by a universally consistent method converges to the expected error of the Bayes Rule. Although this does not guarantee a rate of convergence, it can be shown that no method provides such a guarantee.

3.3.1 Nearest Neighbor Rules

There is a kind of nearest neighbor rule that is universally consistent, although the simplest such rule is not universally consistent.

Recall that data can be represented as labeled points in a feature space. Suppose that a distance measure is defined on that

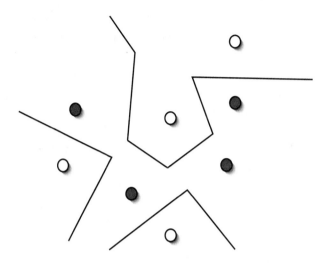

Figure 3.1
Nearest neighbor classification.

space. Then the 1-nearest neighbor method says to classify a new item as having the same category as the nearest datum in the feature space. Any set of n data items then serves to specify the corresponding rule of classification (figure 3.1). As more and more data are obtained, the corresponding rule changes to adapt to the labels on the new items. The 1-nearest neighbor rule is not universally consistent, but it can be shown that in the limit the expected error of the 1-nearest neighbor rule is no more than *twice* the expected error of the Bayes Rule, which is quite good if the Bayes Rule has a very small error rate.

It is possible to do better by using a variant of the 1-nearest neighbor rule. For example, a k-nearest neighbor method says to classify a new item by looking not just at the nearest datum in the feature space but to the k nearest data and assigning to the new item the classification of a majority of those k nearest data. This sometimes (not always) does better than a 1-nearest neighbor rule but is not yet universally consistent.

The key to getting a universally consistent nearest neighbor rule is to let the number of neighbors used grow with n (the amount of data we have) but not too quickly. That is, we let k be a function of n, so this is called a k_n-nearest neighbor rule. We let $k_n \to \infty$ so that we use more and more neighbors as the amount of training data increases. But we also make sure that $\frac{k_n}{n} \to 0$, so that asymptotically the number of neighbors we use is a negligible fraction of the total amount of data. This ensures that we use only neighbors that get closer and closer to the point in feature space that we want to categorize. For example, we might let $k_n = \sqrt{n}$ to satisfy both conditions.

It turns out that with any such k_n (such that $k_n \to \infty$ and $k_n/n \to 0$), in the limit as the amount of training data grows, the performance of the k_n-nearest neighbor rule approaches that of the optimal Bayes Rule, so this sort of k_n-nearest neighbor rule is universally consistent.

Unfortunately, there will always be probability distributions for which the convergence rate is arbitrarily slow. This is different from enumerative induction using a class of rules C of finite VC dimension, where convergence to the best error rate for classification rules in C is not arbitrarily slow and we can specify a function that sets an upper bound on how much data is needed to achieve a certain performance, as we have indicated above. On the other hand, with enumerative induction the rules in C might not contain the Bayes Rule and might not contain a rule with an error rate that is close to the error rate of the Bayes Rule.

3.4 Structural Risk Minimization

We now want to discuss another kind of universally consistent method for using data to select a rule of classification. This alternative to enumerative induction trades off empirical adequacy with respect to data against another factor, sometimes called "simplicity," although that is not always the best name for this factor.

One example of this sort of method, "structural risk minimization" (Vapnik and Chervonenkis 1974), is defined in relation to a class of rules that includes an infinite nesting of classes of rules of finite VC dimension. More precisely, $C = C_1 \cup C_2 \cup \cdots \cup C_n \cup \cdots$, where $C_1 \subset C_2 \subset \cdots \subset C_n \subset \cdots$, and where the VC dimension of C_i is strictly less than the VC dimension of C_j when $i < j$. Any class C of this sort has infinite VC dimension.

Structural risk minimization endorses any rule that minimizes some given function of the empirical error of the rule on the data and the VC-dimension of the smallest class containing the rule. It might, for example, endorse any rule that minimizes the *sum* of these two quantities.

It can be shown that there are many ways to choose these nested classes and the trade-off between fit to data and VC dimension so that structural risk minimization will be universally consistent by endorsing rules that, with probability approaching 1, have expected errors that approach in the limit the expected error of the Bayes Rule.

3.5 Minimum Description Length

Structural risk minimization is one way to balance empirical adequacy with respect to data against some ordering of rules or hypotheses. In that case rules are members of nested classes of finite VC dimension and are ordered by the VC dimension of the smallest class which they belong to. Various other sorts of ordering have been proposed (e.g., Rissanen 1978; Barron et al. 1998; Chaitin 1974; Akaike 1974; Blum and Blum 1975; Gold 1967; Solomonoff 1964).

One alternative type of ordering of rules uses the lengths of their shortest representation in some specified system of representation, for example, the shortest computer program of a certain sort that specifies the relevant labeling of points in the feature space. The class of rules that are represented in this way can have infinite VC dimension, so enumerative induction with its reliance on empirical risk minimization alone will not be effective. But any such ordering of all representable rules can be used by an inductive method that balances the empirical adequacy of a rule on the data against its place in the ordering. Some methods of this sort will in the limit tend to endorse rules with expected error approaching that of the Bayes Rule.

Notice, by the way, that if rules are ordered by minimum description length, it will not be true, for example, that all linear rules $y = ax + b$ have the same place in the ordering, because the parameters a and b must be replaced with descriptions of their values, and, given a fixed system of representation, different values of the parameters will be represented by longer or shorter representations. For this reason, some linear rules will require considerably longer representations than some quadratic rules, which will by this criterion then be treated as "simpler" than those linear rules.

The kind of ordering involved in structural risk minimization is of a somewhat different sort from any kind of ordering by length of representation. Structural risk minimization identifies rules with mathematical functions and is therefore not limited to considering only rules that are finitely represented in a given system. Whereas the number of linear rules conceived as mathematical functions is uncountably infinite, the number of finitely representable linear rules is only countably infinite.

Even apart from that consideration, the ordering that results from structural risk minimization need not be a well-ordering, because it might not have the property that every rule in the ordering has at most only finitely many rules ordered before it. In a typical application of structural risk minimization, infinitely many linear rules are ordered before any nondegenerate quadratic rule. But an ordering of rules by description length can be converted into a well-ordering of rules (by ordering "alphabetically" all rules whose shortest representations have the same length).

3.6   Simplicity

If the ordering against which empirical fit is balanced is supposed to be an ordering in terms of simplicity, one might object that this wrongly assumes that the world is simple. But to use simplicity in this way in inductive reasoning is not to assume the world is simple. What is at issue is comparative simplicity. Induction favors a simpler hypothesis over a less simple hypothesis that fits the data equally well. Given enough data, that preference can lead to the acceptance of very unsimple hypotheses.

3.7   Estimating a Real Variable and Curve Fitting

We have discussed these two sorts of induction as aimed at coming up with rules of classification. Similar results apply to function estimation or curve fitting. Here we review our earlier discussion of estimating the value of a real variable and note how structural risk minimization applies.

In real value estimation, the task is to estimate the value of a variable given the values of each of D observed features. The variable in question may or may not depend on all of the features and may depend on other quantities as well. We assume that there is a background probability distribution that specifies the probability relationship between values of the features and possible observed values of the function. We represent each of the D observable features using a D-dimensional feature space. A possible rule for estimating the value of the variable can be represented as a curve in a $D + 1$ space.

We mentioned a very simple example where $D = 1$ and we are trying to estimate an unknown variable using a single feature. As we have already discussed, any function estimating the variable has an error determined by the background probability distribution.

Each datum can be represented as a point in the plane, where the x coordinate represents the value of the observable feature and the y coordinate represents the value of the variable the datum provides for that observed feature. The task is to estimate the value of the variable for other values of the feature by fitting a curve to the data.

Obviously, infinitely many curves go through all the data (figure 3.2). So there are at least two possible strategies. We can limit the curves to a certain set C, such as the set of straight lines, and choose that curve in C with the least error on the data. Or we can allow many more curves in C and use something like structural risk minimization to select a curve, trying to minimize

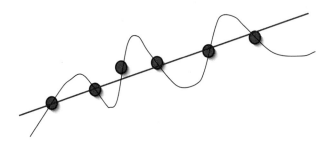

Figure 3.2
Curve fitting.

some function of the empirical error on the data and the complexity of the curve.

We might measure complexity by the VC dimension of the class C, thinking of these curves as the border between YES, too high, and NO, too low.

One might use simple enumerative induction to fit a curve to data points, for example, a linear equation. Or one might balance empirical fit to data against something else, as in structural risk minimization.

3.8 Goodman's New Riddle

The distinction between empirical risk minimization and structural risk minimization sheds light on certain philosophical issues. For one thing, it sheds light on different ways some philosophers have reacted to Nelson Goodman's "new riddle of induction" (Goodman 1953).

As formulated, Goodman's "new riddle" doesn't fit into the standard statistical learning theory paradigm. But there is a reformulation of it that does fit.

We might formulate the original version as follows. The problem is to predict whether a given item is green or not, when it is first observed. In other words, there is a single feature, representing time of first observation, and the feature space is therefore one-dimensional. The data consist in labeled points in this one-dimensional feature space, where each label is either "green" or "not green." We want to use the data to select a function that assigns labels to all points in the feature space. Our goal is to minimize expected error in our predictions about cases as they arise.

This version of the problem does not fit the basic statistical learning theory paradigm in which data are assumed to arise from the same probability distribution as new cases to be predicted. In this first version of Goodman's problem, the relevant feature, time of first observation, is not randomly distributed because there is no chance that the data will assign labels to items first examined later than the current time.

But we can easily modify the problem by taking the relevant feature to be some property of items that we can assume to have the same random distribution in the data and in new cases, for example, the weight or *mass* of the item. Then the data consist in certain pairings of values of measured mass and labels, "green" and "not green." Again we want to use the data to select a function that assigns labels to all possible values for mass, where our goal is to minimize expected error in our predictions about cases as they arise.

Suppose that we want to use enumerative induction with no limit on the hypotheses in C. Of course, if all the data points are labeled "green" and none is labeled "not green," it seems we would want to adopt the hypothesis that all points are to be labeled "green," because that hypothesis has no error on the data. This would lead us to predict that the next item, no matter what its mass, will be correctly labeled "green." However, to adapt Goodman's point in his original formulation of the riddle, there are other hypotheses that correctly fit the data but give different predictions about new items. For example, there will always be a possible hypothesis that says assigns the label "green" to all the *actual* data points and "not green" to all other points. So, the rule of enumerative induction does not give useful advice about cases whose values of the relevant feature differ from any data points.

From this, Goodman concludes that we cannot allow enumerative induction to treat all possible hypotheses equally. In our terms, there must be limits on C. Furthermore, Goodman assumes that there is a unique class of hypotheses C, consisting in those hypotheses that are "confirmed" by their instances. The "new riddle of induction" is then the problem of characterizing the relevant class of hypotheses, C, the confirmable or lawlike hypotheses. Goodman attempts to advance a solution to this problem (a) by characterizing a class of "projectible" predicates in terms of the extent to which these predicates have been used to make successful predictions in the past, and (b) by giving principles that explain the confirmability of a hypothesis in terms of the projectibility of the predicates in which it is expressed.

Goodman argues that projectible predicates cannot be identified with those predicates for which we have a single word, like "green" as opposed to "green if mass of 15, 24, 33, . . . and not green otherwise," because we could use a single word "grue" for the latter predicate. He argues that projectible predicates cannot be identified with directly observational predicates, like "green," because we can envision a machine that can directly observe whether something is "grue." Goodman himself suggests that the projectible predicates can be characterized in terms of the extent to which these predicates have been used to make successful predictions in the past.

Statistical learning theory takes a very different approach. It does not attempt to solve this "new riddle of induction." It does not attempt to distinguish those predicates that are really projectible from those that are not, and it does not attempt to distinguish those hypotheses that are really confirmable from their instances from those that are not.

Of course, statistical learning theory does accept the moral that induction requires inductive bias among hypotheses. But it does not attempt to specify a unique class C of confirmable hypotheses. In the case of enumerative induction, statistical learning theory says only that the set C of hypotheses to be considered must have finite VC dimension. In the case of structural risk minimization, statistical learning theory requires a certain structure on the set of hypotheses being considered. Statistical learning theory does not attempt to specify which particular hypotheses are to be included in the set C, nor where particular hypotheses appear in the structures needed for structural risk minimization.

Goodman's riddle has received extensive discussion by philosophers (some collected in Stalker 1994 and Elgin 1997). While many authors suppose that the solution to the new riddle of induction requires specifying some relevant class of projectible hypotheses, others have argued instead that what is needed is an account of "degrees of projectibility," where for example intuitively simpler hypotheses count as more projectible than intuitively more complex hypotheses.

One observation about these two interpretations of the riddle is that the first, with its emphasis on restricting induction to a special class of projectible hypotheses, involves identifying induction with enumerative induction, conceived as empirical risk minimization, with the advantages and disadvantages of considering only rules from a class of rules with finite VC dimension. The second interpretation, with its emphasis on degrees of projectibility, can allow consideration of rules from a class of rules with infinite VC dimension. It can do this by abandoning simple enumerative induction in favor of structural risk minimization or some other way of balancing data-coverage against simplicity or projectibility.

Philosophers discussing Goodman's new riddle have not fully appreciated that these two ways of approaching the new riddle of induction involve different kinds of inductive methods, empirical risk minimization on the one hand and methods that balance fit to data against something else on the other hand.

One philosophically useful thing about the analysis of inductive reasoning in statistical learning theory is the way it sheds light on the difference between these two interpretations of Goodman's new riddle.

3.9 Popper on Simplicity

We now want to say something more about Popper's (1934, 1979) discussion of scientific method. We noted earlier that Popper argues that there is no justification for any sort of inductive reasoning, but he does think that there are justified scientific methods.

In particular, he argues that a version of structural risk minimization best captures actual scientific method (although of course he does not use the term "structural risk minimization").

In his view, scientists accept a certain ordering of classes of hypotheses, an ordering based on the number of *parameters* needing to be specified to be able to pick out a particular member of the class. So, for example, for real value estimation on the basis of one feature, linear hypotheses of the form $y = ax + b$ have two parameters, a and b; quadratic hypotheses of the form $y = ax^2 + bx + c$ have three parameters, a, b, and c; and so forth. So, linear hypotheses are ordered before quadratic hypotheses, and so forth.

Popper takes this ordering to be based on "falsifiability" in the sense that at least three data points are needed to "falsify" a claim that the relevant function is linear, at least four are needed to "falsify" the claim that the relevant function is quadratic, and so forth.

As explained in chapter 2, in Popper's somewhat misleading terminology, data "falsify" a hypothesis by being inconsistent with it, so that the hypothesis has positive empirical error on the data. He recognizes, however, that actual data do not show that a hypothesis is false, because the data themselves might be noisy and so not strictly speaking correct.

Popper takes the ordering of classes of hypotheses in terms of parameters to be an ordering in terms of "simplicity" in one important sense of that term. So, he takes it that scientists balance data-coverage against simplicity, where simplicity is measured by "falsifiability" (Popper 1934, section 43).

We can distinguish several claims here.

(1) Hypothesis choice requires an ordering of nested classes of hypotheses.

(2) This ordering represents the degree of "falsifiability" of a given class of hypotheses.

(3) Classes are ordered in accordance with the number of parameters whose values need to be specified in order to pick out specific hypotheses.

(4) The ordering ranks *simpler* hypotheses before more *complex* hypotheses.

Claim (1) is also part of structural risk minimization. Claim (2) is similar to the appeal to VC dimension in structural risk minimization, except that Popper's degree of falsifiability does not coincide with VC dimension, as noted in chapter 2 above. As we will see in a moment, claim (3) is inadequate and, interpreted as Popper does, it is incompatible with (2) and with structural risk minimization. Claim (4) is at best terminological and may be just wrong.

Claim (3) is inadequate because there can be many ways to specify the same class of hypotheses, using different numbers of parameters. For example, linear hypotheses in the plane might be represented as instances of $abx + cd$, with four parameters instead of two. Alternatively, notice that it is possible to code a pair of real numbers a, b as a single real number c, so that a and b can be recovered from c. That is, there are functions such that $f(a, b) = c$, where $f_1(c) = a$ and $f_2(c) = b$.[2] Given such a coding, we can represent linear hypotheses as $f_1(c)x + f_2(c)$ using only the one parameter c. In fact, for any class of hypotheses that can be represented using P parameters, there is another way to represent the same class of hypotheses using only one parameter.

Perhaps Popper means claim (3) to apply to some ordinary or preferred way of representing classes in terms of parameters, so that the representations using the above coding functions do

2. For example, f might take the decimal representations of a and b and interleave them to get c.

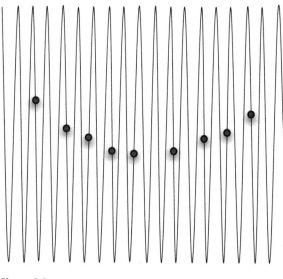

Figure 3.3
Real variable estimation using sine curves.

not count. But even if we use ordinary representations, claim (3) conflicts with claim (2) and with structural risk minimization.

To see this, consider the class of sine curves $y = a \sin(bx)$. For almost every set of n consistent data points (which do not assign different y values to the same x value) there will be sine curves coming arbitrarily close to those points (figure 3.3). In that sense, the class of sine curves has infinite "falsifiability" in Popper's sense even though only two parameters have to be specified to determine a particular member of the set, using the sort of representation Popper envisioned. Popper himself did not realize this and explicitly treats the class of sine curves as relatively simple in the relevant respect (1934, Section 44).

The class of sine curves can also be seen to have infinite VC dimension if we think of the curves as rules for classifying points as "too high" or "not too high," because for any N there will be a set of N points that is shattered by the class of sine curves. That is, members of that class can provide the 2^N possible classifications of the N points.

The fact that the class of sine curves has infinite VC dimension, as well as infinite falsifiability in Popper's sense, is some evidence that the relevant ordering of hypotheses for scientific hypothesis acceptance is not a simplicity ordering, at least if sine curves count as "simple."

3.10 Empirically Equivalent Rules

Finally, we consider whether empirically equivalent hypotheses must always be treated in the same way in statistical learning theory. In particular, what about scientific hypotheses in comparison with empirically equivalent skeptical hypotheses?

Suppose two hypotheses, H and G, are empirically equivalent. For example, where H is some highly regarded scientific hypothesis, let G be the corresponding demonic hypothesis that a powerful godlike demon has arranged that the data you get will be exactly as expected if H were true. Could simplicity as analyzed in statistical learning theory provide a reason to accept H rather than G?

One might suppose that the answer is "no," because the kinds of analyses provided by statistical learning theory concern how to minimize expected errors, and these two hypotheses make exactly the same predictions. Indeed, if we identify the hypotheses with their predictions, they are the same hypothesis.

But it isn't obvious that hypotheses that make the same predictions should be identified. The way a hypothesis is represented suggests what class of hypotheses it belongs to for purposes of assessing simplicity. Different representations suggest different classes. Even mathematically equivalent hypotheses might be treated differently within statistical learning theory. The class of linear hypotheses, $f(x) = ax + b$, is simpler than the class of quadratic hypotheses, $f(x) = ax^2 + bx + c$, on various measures—number of parameters, VC dimension, and so on. If the first parameter of a quadratic hypothesis is 0, the hypothesis is mathematically equivalent to a linear hypothesis. But its linear representation belongs to a simpler class than the quadratic representation. So for purposes of choice of rule, there is reason to count the linear representation as simpler than the quadratic representation.

Similarly, although H and G yield the same predictions, there is a sense in which they are not contained in the same hypothesis classes. We might say that H falls into a class of hypotheses with a better simplicity ranking than G, perhaps because the class containing H has a lower VC dimension than the class containing G. The relevant class containing G might contain any hypothesis of the form, "The data will be exactly as expected as if ϕ were true," where ϕ ranges over all possible scientific hypothesis. Since ϕ has infinite VC dimension, so does this class containing G. From this perspective, there is reason to prefer H over G even though they are empirically equivalent.

So, in fact we may have reason to think that we are not living in the Matrix (Wachowski and Wachowski 1999)!

3.11 Important Ideas from Statistical Learning Theory

Here are some of the ideas from statistical learning theory that we have discussed so far which we believe are philosophically and methodologically important.

Statistical learning theory provides a way of thinking about the reliability of a rule of classification in terms of expected cost or expected error, where that presupposes a background statistical probability distribution.

With respect to rules of classification, there is the notion of the Bayes Rule, the most reliable rule, the rule with the least expected error or expected cost.

The goodness of an inductive method is to be measured in terms of the reliability of the classification rules the method comes up with.

Useful inductive methods require some inductive bias, either as reflected in a restriction in the rules in C or as a preference for some rules in C over others.

There is the idea of shattering, as capturing a kind of notion of falsifiability, and the corresponding notion of VC dimension.

There is the contrast between uniform convergence of error rates and universal consistency.

In the next chapter we will discuss some additional ideas from statistical learning theory and consider their significance for psychology and cognitive science as well as for philosophy.

3.12 Summary

In this chapter, we compared enumerative induction with methods that also take into account some ordering of hypotheses. We discussed how these methods apply to classification and to real variable estimation or curve fitting. We compared two different methods for balancing data-coverage against an ordering of hypotheses in terms of simplicity or some simplicity substitute. We noted that there are two ways to respond to Goodman's (1965) new riddle of induction, corresponding to these two kinds of inductive method. We also discussed some of Karl Popper's ideas about scientific method, trying to distinguish what is right and what is wrong about these ideas. Finally, we considered how appeal to simplicity or some similar ordering might provide a principled way to prefer one hypothesis over another skeptical hypothesis that is empirically equivalent with it.

4 Neural Networks, Support Vector Machines, and Transduction

4.1 Introduction

In our three previous chapters we discussed methods of induction that arrive at general rules of classification on the basis of empirical data. We contrasted enumerative induction with nearest neighbor induction and with methods of induction that balance empirical risk against some sort of ordering of hypotheses, including structural risk minimization in which classes of hypotheses are ordered by their VC dimension. We compared results about these methods with philosophical discussions by Nelson Goodman and Karl Popper.

In this final chapter, we briefly sketch some applications of statistical learning theory to machine learning, including perceptrons, feed-forward neural networks, and support vector machines. We consider whether support vector machines might provide a useful psychological model for human categorization. We describe recent research on "transduction." Where induction uses labeled data to come up with rules of classification, transduction also uses the information that certain new unlabeled cases have come up.

The theory of transduction suggests new models of how people sometimes reason. The hypothesis that people sometimes reason transductively provides a possible explanation of some psychological data that have been interpreted as showing that people are inconsistent or irrational. It also provides a possible account of a certain sort of "moral particularism."

4.2   Machine Learning: Perceptrons

A *rule of classification* assigns a classification to each point in a certain feature space. Let us consider in particular the simplest case in which the classification has two possible values, YES and NO, which might be represented by outputting 1 or 0.

Learning machines use data in order to implement classification rules. Some learning machines begin with a more or less randomly chosen classification rule which is then modified in light of the data. Sometimes it is appropriate to think of the data being used to "train" the learning machine.

A *perceptron* (figure 4.1) is a learning machine with D inputs, one for each of the D observable features an object can have.

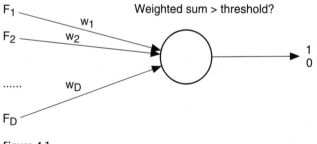

Figure 4.1
Perceptron.

The perceptron takes a weighted sum of its inputs, and outputs 1 if this sum is greater than a specified *threshold* and 0 if it is not.

The particular classification rule implemented by a perceptron is determined by a set of weights indicating the strength of the connection between each input and the perceptron. There is a simple perceptron learning procedure. The perceptron is trained by using data to suggest changes of the weights of the input connections. Before learning, the weights on the inputs are assigned random values (positive and negative). For each datum, the values of its features are input to the perceptron. If the perceptron outputs the correct classification of the datum, no change is made in the input weights. If the perceptron outputs the wrong classification, the weights on the inputs are changed slightly in a particular way in order to make the weighted sum of the inputs closer to the desired value. This procedure can be repeated by going through the data as many times as needed.

If the data can all be correctly classified by some perceptron, this perceptron learning procedure will eventually lead to a collection of input connection weights that allows the perceptron to classify all the data correctly. Once the data have been correctly classified, the weights are fixed and the perceptron is used to classify new cases.

The qualification "if the data can all be correctly classified by some perceptron" is a significant limitation on this result, because it is easy to see that a perceptron can only represent linearly separable classifications. Any given perceptron outputs a YES if and only if the inputs satisfy the following condition, where the F_i represent the values of the features, the w_i represent the weights of those inputs, and T represents the threshold.

$$w_1F_1 + w_2F_2 + \cdots + w_DF_D > T$$

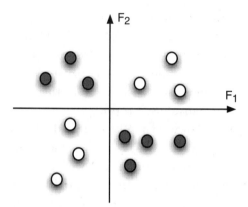

Figure 4.2
XOR of F_1 and F_2.

The equation for the separation between the YESes and the NOs can be expressed simply by changing the ">" to "=":

$$w_1F_1 + w_2F_2 + \cdots + w_DF_D = T$$

which is a linear equation, in D variables, representing a hyperplane in the D-dimensional feature space.

Recall that linearly separable classifications are very limited and cannot for example represent the XOR classification (figure 4.2). An XOR classifier with two inputs, F_1 and F_2, indicates YES or 1 if $F_1F_2 \leq 0$ and NO or 0 if $F_1F_2 > 0$. A perceptron classifier cannot serve as an XOR classifier, because the YES region cannot be separated from the NO region by a straight line.

It follows of course that, since there cannot be a perceptron classifier that correctly represents XOR, data cannot be used to *train* a perceptron classifier to represent XOR.

Recall that the VC dimension of rules represented by a perceptron classifier is $D + 1$, where D is the number of dimensions in the feature space (that is, the number of features whose values are points in the space). This is a finite number, so the strong learning result mentioned in the second chapter applies. There is a specifiable function that indicates how much data is needed to find a rule with such and such a probability of an error rate that is within a certain approximation to the best linear rule. On the other hand, linear classifiers have very limited representational power.

4.3   Feed-Forward Neural Networks

Feed-forward neural networks address the problem of limited representational power by combining several *layers* of perceptrons, the outputs from earlier layers serving as inputs to the perceptrons in later layers (figure 4.3).

For any rule of classification there is a three-layer network that approximates it to whatever accuracy is desired, given enough nodes per layer.

To see that this is so, recall that any rule of classification is equivalent to a specification of those points in feature space that are to be classified as YESes (or 1s). Those points are contained in the union of some set of (convex) hypervolumes of the feature space. Each such hypervolume can be approximated by a (convex) volume with hyperplanes as sides (figure 4.4). A different perceptron can be used to capture each of the hyperplane classifications (figure 4.5). The outputs of these perceptrons can then be sent to a downstream AND perceptron that captures the hypervolume by outputting 1 iff all of its inputs are 1. The same thing is done for each of the other hypervolumes. Their outputs are sent to a final OR perceptron that

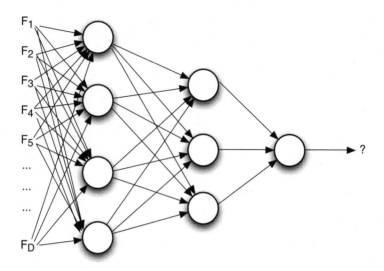

Figure 4.3
A feed-forward network.

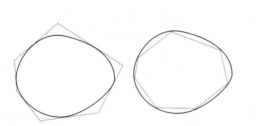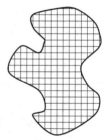

Figure 4.4
Approximating a convex hypervolume.

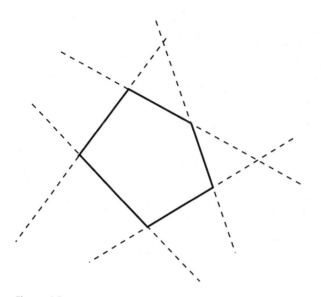

Figure 4.5
Intersecting half-spaces.

outputs 1 iff at least one of its inputs is 1 (figure 4.6). The whole system then approximates the intended rule of classification.

We have been supposing that a perceptron outputs a 1 iff the weighted sum of its inputs exceeds a certain threshold. This is a *sharp* threshold in the sense that a slight change in the weighted sum of the inputs can make a dramatic change in what is output by the perceptron. For learning using a feed-forward network of perceptrons, it is useful to replace the sharp threshold of the perceptrons with a more continuous (S-shaped) threshold. (Then, to obtain a 0/1 classification, the final output is passed through a sharp threshold.) Then, for example, a learning rule using *back propagation of error* often works well in practice. We will not try

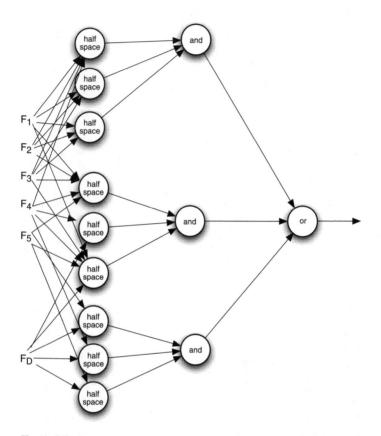

Figure 4.6
Taking a union of intersections.

to explain this further here. Instead we turn to a different response to the problem of limited representational power.

4.4 Support Vector Machines

Support vector machines (SVMs) provide an alternative response to the limitations of perceptrons (Vapnik 1998, part II; 2000, pp. 139ff; Hastie et al. 2001, pp. 371–389). Instead of adding additional layers to the network, SVMs begin by mapping the data into a higher-dimensional space in which the data can be more nearly linearly separated than in the original space. So, for example, the data in the XOR problem might be mapped into a three-dimensional space in such a way that each point F_1, F_2 is mapped onto F_1, F_2, F_3, where $F_3 = F_1 F_2$. The transformed data points are linearly separable in that three-dimensional space by the plane perpendicular to the F_3 axis at $F_3 = 0$, that is, the plane defined by the F_1 and F_2 axes, because the YES items are below that plane and the NO items are above it (figure 4.7).

Usually, in practice, many different hyperplanes separate the data in the transformed higher-dimensional space. The data points that touch the space occupied by the separating hyperplanes are called "support vectors."

In one SVM approach, the hyperplane that *maximally* separates the data (as represented by its distance from the set of "support vectors") is chosen to separate the YESes from the NOs. The equation of the chosen maximally separating hyperplane can then be used to find the corresponding equation in the original feature space to separate the YESes from NOs in that space.

In the XOR example, if the chosen rule in the transformed space is that YESes are those points for which $F_3 < 0$, then,

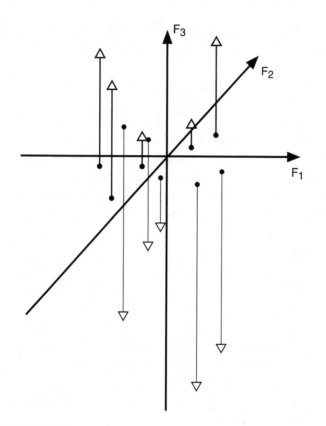

Figure 4.7

Mapping 2D XOR into 3D. The arrows point to where points in the F_1 F_2 plane are mapped to 3D-space.

recalling that the transformation from the original feature space is sets $F_3 = F_1F_2$ we get the result that the YESes are those points for which $F_1F_2 < 0$.

Different support vector machines use different mappings from the original feature space to a higher-dimensional space. The larger space will normally contain dimensions for all the original features along with further dimensions representing various products of the features with each other and themselves. For example, starting with just two features F_1 and F_2, there could be three other features, $F_3 = F_1F_2$, $F_4 = F_1^2$, and $F_5 = F_1^2F_2$. Linear separations in the larger space then correspond to algebraic rules in the original feature space. The rules represented by any such support vector machine will have a finite VC dimension, because the VC dimension of linear separations in a finite dimensional space is finite.

It is possible to envision a support vector machine that maps the original feature space to an infinite dimensional space with dimensions for all possible products of powers of the original features, so that every algebraic rule is represented by a linear separation in that infinite dimensional space.

Of course, the VC dimension of the linear separations in an infinite dimensional space is infinite. But if all cases of interest are confined to a hypersphere with a finite radius and can be separated with a hyperslab of a certain thickness or "margin," the relevant VC-like dimension is finite (Vapnik 2000, pp. 132–133).

Feed-forward neural networks can be seen as a special case of the idea of mapping the original feature space into another in which the data can be linearly separated. The earlier parts of the network map the original feature space into another which is linearly separated by the final unit (Vapnik 2000, p. 3).

4.5   Psychology and Support Vectors

Support vector machines represent categories through their support vectors, which determine the borders of the category. It is interesting to consider to what extent human categorization uses a similar representation.

There is considerable evidence that people represent categories in terms of paradigm central exemplars, the paradigm dog or the paradigm bird, for example, which would seem to be rather different from the sort of representation used by support vector machines.

But studies of "categorical perception" provide evidence that people are indeed also sensitive to category boundaries. Differences among items of different categories seem greater than differences among items of the same category. As Harnad (1987) explains this:

An example of [categorical perception] is the color spectrum as it is subdivided into color categories, or an acoustic continuum called the second-formant transition as it is subdivided into the stop-consonant categories /ba/, /da/ and /ga/. In both cases, equal-sized physical differences between stimuli are perceived as larger or smaller depending on whether the stimuli are in the same category or different ones. Indeed, the effect is not only quantitative but qualitative: A pair of greens of different shades look more like one another than like a shade of yellow (which may be no more different in wave length from one of the greens than the other green is), and this difference is one of quality. The same is true of /ba/'s and /da/'s.

In other words, people do sometimes make distinctions that have to do with the edges of categories and not just their central exemplars. This is predicted by the hypothesis that category representation is a kind of SVM representation.

At this point, we're getting into issues about vague and possibly shifting boundaries (Fara 2000). What exactly do we represent? We don't represent the edges of the concept, because if we did there would be no vagueness. We represent certain near-borderline cases to which we take the concept to apply and perhaps other cases to which we take it not to apply.

4.6   Transduction

The inductive learning methods we have considered so far all involve using labeled data to find a rule that is then used to classify new cases as they arise.

Furthermore, these methods all involve learning total classifications. Nearest neighbor methods, perceptrons, multilayer feed-forward networks, and standard SVMs all yield rules that assign a classification to every possible set of features.

We could modify some of these methods to provide only partial classifications. For example, we could modify SVMs not to choose among the various separating hyperplanes in the space between the support vectors. The points in this in-between space would be left unclassified. The system would still be an inductive method, since it would classify some, perhaps many, new cases in accordance with a rule derived from labeled data, but the rule would not be a total rule, since it would not characterize points in the in-between space.

Suppose we are using a method that in this way provides only a partial classification of cases, and a case arises to be classified in the intervening space between support vectors. Vapnik (1979, 1998, 2000) considers certain *transductive* methods for classifying such new cases, methods that use information about what new cases have come up to be classified and then select a subset of separations that (a) correctly classify the data and (b) agree on their classifications of the new cases. In one version, the selected separations also (c) disagree as much as possible on the classifications of other possible cases.

An important related version of transduction uses not only the information that certain new cases have come up to be classified but also the information that there is a certain set U ("universum") of examples that are hard to classify. In this version, transduction selects the subset of linear separations that satisfy (a) and (b) but disagree as much as possible on the classification of the hard cases in U.

Transduction performs considerably better than other methods in certain difficult real-life situations involving high-dimensional feature spaces where there is relatively little data (Joachims 1999; Weston et al. 2003; Goutte et al. 2004).

4.7   Transduction and Induction

Vapnik (2000, p. 293) says that transduction does not involve first inferring an *inductive generalization* which is then used for classification. On the other hand, Harman (1965, 1967) argues that any such inference should always be treated as a special case of *inference to the best explanation* where the relevant sort of explanation appeals to a generalization. There is an apparent conflict here, but on analysis the conflict appears to be terminological.

Transduction differs from the other inductive methods we have been discussing in this way: the classification of new cases is not always based on an inductive generalization from labeled data. So, transduction does not involve *that sort of inductive gen-*

eralization. That is because transduction makes use of the information that certain new cases have come up to be assessed.

On the other hand, transduction does involve the implicit acceptance of a nontotal generalization P, corresponding to the selected subset of separations in the transformed higher-dimensional space. So, transduction does involve inductive generalization in a wider sense, even if not inductive generalization from the labeled data alone.

It is true that, although the data include what new cases have come up, the classifications that transduction gives to these new cases are not treated as data. When additional new cases arise, transduction applied to the old plus the new cases can modify the classifications. It might therefore be said that the principle P derived from accepting the new classifications is hostage to the new cases in a way that inductive generalizations from labeled data are not. But transduction treats the fact that certain new cases have come up as data, and new data always have the potential to change which rule should be accepted.

In other words, there is a sense in which transduction does not involve inductive generalization, because the relevant generalization is not arrived at from the labeled data alone, and there is a sense in which transduction does involve inductive generalization, because it does arrive at a general rule based on labeled data plus information about what new cases have come up.

What is important and not merely terminological is that, under certain conditions, transduction gives considerably better results in practice than those obtained from methods that use labeled data to infer a rule which is then used to classify new cases (Joachims 1999; Vapnik 2000; Weston et al. 2003; Goutte et al. 2004).

4.8   Do People Use Transduction?

It is an interesting question whether people ever use something like transduction. As far as we know, psychologists have not addressed this question, which is not surprising given that the theory of transduction is of such recent origin.

It is true that people often categorize something without being able to formulate a relevant principle of categorization. But that by itself is compatible with their judging on the basis of a general principle. They might be using an unconscious or implicit principle. Suppose they reach conclusions using something like feed-forward neural networks. Such networks encode principles in their connection weights and there is no reason to expect people to have access to the relevant principles.

What evidence might bear on the question of whether and when people use transduction? Notice that how transduction will categorize a new case can depend on what other new cases have come up. Feed-forward neural networks and other inductive methods do not have this feature. But as psychologists have amply documented, the way a person categorizes a new case often does depend on what other new cases are to be categorized. Psychologists often suggest that this illustrates "irrationality" in human thinking, a "framing effect," perhaps. But it may indicate instead that people sometimes reason transductively.

Gladwell (2005) describes many cases in which people reach judgments in "the blink of an eye," judgments that do not seem to be derived from any sort of general principle and that are quite sensitive to what they have been thinking about immediately before making the judgment. It is possible that these examples are also instances of some sort of transduction.

Redelmeier and Shafir (1995) discuss the following sort of example. Suppose that a certain painful condition can be alleviated by either of two medicines, each of which has different side effects. If only one is available, doctors tend to prescribe it for this condition. If both are available, doctors tend to prescribe neither, presumably because they have difficulty deciding between them. Redelmeier and Shafir treat this as an example of irrationality; but perhaps it merely illustrates a feature of transductive inference, namely, that the categorization of an item depends on what other items there are to be categorized.

Similarly, customers who come upon a display of six jams are more apt to decide to purchase one of the jams than are customers who come upon a display of twenty-four jams including those six (Iyengar and Lepper 2000). The task of deciding between all twenty-four jams is presumably too difficult to be worth the cost. Schwartz (2004) discusses other similar examples. Again there is the question of whether such examples are the result of transduction.

Recall too that one promising transductive method includes in the data that there is a set U of examples that are hard to classify. This version of transduction selects the subset of linear separations that (a) correctly classify the data, (b) agree on their classifications of the new cases, and (c) disagree as much as possible on the classification of the hard cases in U.

Superior courts sometimes seem to reason in this way by trying to resolve a case at hand in the narrowest possible way so as minimize the impact of the decision on other hard cases. Of course, because of the role of precedent in the law, these decisions differ from typical cases of transductive categorization, which (as we have noted) set no precedent, although the general theory of transduction can be extended to cover this sort of case also.

Courts will say that they do not want to rule on issues that have not been argued before them. But, of course, given the doctrine of precedent, they often do rule on issues that have not been specifically argued before them. When courts say this, it is presumably because they have in mind a certain class of hard cases U which they would rather not decide without further argument. This makes sense from the point of view of the version of transduction that considers the case in which there is such a set of examples U and tries to choose a classification of the new cases that have come up that minimally decides cases in U. (However, as remarked earlier, in the general case conclusions arrived at via transduction are not treated as precedents and may be abandoned as new cases arise.)

4.9 Moral Particularism

The theory of transduction might also be relevant to recent discussions of at least one form of "moral particularism" as opposed to "moral generalism" (see, e.g., Dancy 1993; Sinnott-Armstrong 1999; Hooker and Little 2000; Kihlbom 2002; Väyrynen 2004).

An epistemic version of moral generalism holds that the acceptance of a moral judgment is justified only if it is seen as an instance of a justified general moral principle. A corresponding moral particularism holds that a moral judgment about a particular case can be justified without being seen as an instance of a justified moral principle.

The issues between particularism and generalism are metaphysical, to the extent that they concern the source of moral truths, and epistemic (or psychological) to the extent that they concern the source of reasonable or justified moral decisions and beliefs.

The metaphysical and epistemic issues are possibly connected. Metaphysical moral particularism is often defended by appeal to the claim that for an act to be morally wrong is for it to be such as to be seen or judged wrong by a competent moral judge (Wiggins 1998; McDowell 1998), plus the claim that epistemic moral particularism applies to the competent moral judge.

Harman (2005) argues that the theory of transduction supports a weak form of epistemic moral particularism. We now have doubts about that argument, but the issue is too complex for us to discuss here. In any event, some reasoning that appears to support epistemic moral particularism may involve moral transduction.

4.10   Summary

In this book, we have argued that statistical learning theory is highly relevant to issues in philosophy and psychology.

In our first chapter, we treated the problem of induction as the problem of assessing the *reliability* of inductive methods. Although the problem is sometimes motivated by comparing induction with deduction, we argued that such a comparison rests on a confusion about the relation between inference and logic. We noted suggestions that the only real problem is to say how we actually reason inductively. We considered the idea that the question of reliability can be answered by adjusting one's methods and beliefs so that they fit together in a reflective equilibrium. We argued that, although there is evidence that people do reason by adjusting their opinions in the way suggested, there is considerable evidence that the results are fragile and unreliable, and we pointed out that it is hard to be in reflective equilibrium if one cannot believe one's methods of reasoning are reliable.

Our second chapter described how statistical learning theory is concerned with assessing inductive methods that use data to arrive at a reliable rule for classifying new cases on the basis of certain values of features of those new cases. This approach to learning uses the notion of a D-dimensional "feature space," each point in the feature space representing a certain set of feature values. The approach assumes that an unknown probability distribution is responsible for encounters with objects and for the correlations between feature values of objects and their correct classifications. The probability distribution determines the best rule of classification, namely the Bayes Rule that minimizes expected error.

For the special case of a YES/NO classification, we identified a classification rule with a set of points in feature space, perhaps certain disjoint areas or hypervolumes. For example, linear rules divide the space into two regions separated by a line or plane or hyperplane.

Enumerative induction endorses that rule or those rules from a certain set C of rules that minimize error on the data. If enumerative induction is to be useful at all, there have to be significant limits on the rules included in C. So C may fail to contain any rule with expected error comparable to the Bayes Rule. So, we cannot expect enumerative induction to endorse a rule with expected error close to the Bayes Rule. At best it will endorse a rule with expected error close to the minimum for rules in C. And, in fact, we have to settle for its probably endorsing a rule close to the minimum for rules in C.

Vapnik and Chervonenkis (1968) show that no matter what the background probability distribution, with probability approaching 1, as more and more data are considered, the expected error of the rules that enumerative induction endorses will approach the minimum expected error of rules in C *if and only if* the rules in C have a finite VC dimension.

VC dimension is explained in terms of shattering. Rules in C shatter a set of N data points if and only if for every possible labeling of the N points with YESes and NOs, there is a rule in C that perfectly fits that labeling.

In other words, there is no way to label those N points in a way that would falsify the claim that the rules in C are perfectly adequate. This pointed to a possible relationship between the role of VC dimension in learning by enumerative induction and the role of falsifiability in Karl Popper's methodology, a relationship we discussed further in our third chapter.

In that third chapter, we compared enumerative induction with methods that take into account some ordering of hypotheses, perhaps by simplicity. We noted that there are two ways to respond to Goodman's (1965) new riddle of induction, corresponding to these two kinds of inductive method. We discussed how these methods apply to the estimation of the value of a real variable and curve fitting. We compared two different methods for balancing data-coverage against an ordering of hypotheses in terms of simplicity or some simplicity substitute. We also discussed some of Karl Popper's ideas about falsifiability, simplicity, and scientific method. Finally, we considered how appeal to simplicity or some similar ordering might provide a principled way to prefer one hypothesis over another skeptical hypothesis that is empirically equivalent with it.

In this final chapter, we briefly sketched applications of statistical learning theory to perceptrons, feed-forward neural networks, and support vector machines. We considered briefly whether support vector machines might provide a useful psychological model for human categorization. Finally we discussed "transduction," a learning method that uses certain additional information beyond labeled data—information about hard cases and about what cases have come up to be classified. The theory of transduction suggests new models of how people sometimes reason. The hypothesis that people sometimes reason transductively provides a possible explanation of some psychological data that typically have been interpreted as showing that people are inconsistent or irrational. It also provides a possible account of a certain sort of "moral particularism."

References

Akaike, H. (1974). "A New Look at the Statistical Model Identification." *IEEE Transactions on Automatic Control* AC-19: 716–723.

Barron, A., Rissanen, J., and Yu, B. (1998). "The Minimum Description Length Principle in Coding and Modeling." *IEEE Transactions on Information Theory* 44: 2743–2760.

Bishop, M. A., and Trout, J. D. (2005). *Epistemology and the Psychology of Human Judgment.* Oxford: Oxford University Press.

Blum, L., and Blum, M. (1975). "Toward a Mathematical Theory of Inductive Inference." *Information and Control* 28: 125–155.

Bongard, M. (1970). *Pattern Recognition.* Washington, D.C.: Spartan Books.

Burge, T. (1993). "Content Preservation." *Philosophical Review* 102: 457–488.

Chaitin, G. J. (1974). "Information-Theoretic Computational Complexity." *IEEE Transactions on Information Theory* IT-20: 10–15.

Chomsky, N. (1968). *Language and Mind.* New York: Harcourt, Brace, and World.

Chomsky, N. (1981). *Lectures on Government and Binding.* Dordrecht: Foris.

Corfield, D., Schölkopf, B., and Vapnik, V. (2005). "Popper, Falsification, and the VC-dimension." Technical Report No. 145. Max Planck Institute for Biological Cybernetics, Tübingen, Germany.

Cullicover, P. W. (1997). *Principles and Parameters: An Introduction to Syntatic Theory*. Oxford: Oxford University Press.

Dancy, J. (1993). *Moral Reasons*. Oxford: Blackwell.

Daniels, N. (1979). "Wide Reflective Equilibrium and Theory Acceptance in Ethics." *Journal of Philosophy* 76: 256–282.

Descartes, R. (1641). *Meditationes de Prima Philosophia*. Paris.

Duda, R. O., Hart, P. E., and Stork, D. G. (2001). *Pattern Classification*, second edition. New York: Wiley.

Elgin, C. (1997). *Nelson Goodman's New Riddle of Induction: The Philosophy of Nelson Goodman*, volume 2. New York: Garland.

Fara, D. G. (2000). "Shifting Sands: An Interest-Relative Theory of Vagueness." *Philosophical Topics* 28: 45–81. Originally published under the name "Delia Graff."

Feldman, J. A. (1981). "A Connectionist Model of Visual Memory." In G. E. Hinton and J. A. Anderson (eds.), *Parallel Models of Associative Memory*, 49–81. Hillsdale, N.J.: Erlbaum.

Foley, R. (1994). "Egoism in Epistemology." In F. Schmitt (ed.), *Socializing Epistemology*. Lanham: Rowman and Littlefield.

Gladwell, M. (2005). *Blink: The Power of Thinking without Thinking*. New York: Little, Brown.

Gold, E. M. (1967). "Language Identification in the Limit." *Information and Control* 10: 447–474.

Goodman, N. (1953). *Fact, Fiction, and Forecast*. Cambridge, Mass.: Harvard University Press.

Goutte, C., Cancedda, N., Gaussier, E., Dèjean, H. (2004). "Generative vs. Discriminative Approaches to Entity Extraction from Label Deficient

Data." *JADT 2004, 7es Journ'ees internationales d'Analyse statistique des Donn'ees Textuelles.* Louvain-la-Neuve, Belgium, 10–12 March.

Hacking, I. (1965). *The Logic of Statistical Inference.* Cambridge: Cambridge University Press.

Harman, G. (1965). "The Inference to the Best Explanation." *Philosophical Review* 74: 88–95.

Harman, G. (1967). "Enumerative Induction as Inference to the Best Explanation." *Journal of Philosophy* 64: 529–533.

Harman, G. (2005). "Moral Particularism and Transduction." *Philosophical Issues* 15: 44–55.

Harnad, S. (1987). "Psychophysical and Cognitive Aspects of Categorical Perception: A Critical Overview." In S. Harnad (ed.), *Categorical Perception: The Groundwork of Cognition.* New York: Cambridge University Press.

Hastie, T., Tibshirani, R., and Friedman, J. (2001). *The Elements of Statistical Learning: Data Mining, Inference, and Prediction.* New York: Springer.

Holyoak, K. J., and Simon, D. (1999). "Bidirectional Reasoning in Decision Making by Constraint Satisfaction." *Journal of Experimental Psychology: General* 128: 3–31.

Hooker, B., and Little, M. (2000). *Moral Particularism.* New York: Oxford University Press.

Iyengar, S. S., and Lepper, M. R. (2000). "When Choice Is Demotivating: Can One Desire Too Much of a Good Thing?" *Journal of Personality and Social Psychology* 79: 995–1006.

Joachims, T. (1999). "Transductive Inference for Text Classification Using Support Vector Machines." In I. Bratko and S. Dzeroski (eds.), *Proceedings of the 16th International Conference on Machine Learning,* 200–209. San Francisco: Morgan Kaufmann.

Kihlbom, U. (2002). *Ethical Particularism.* Stockhold Studies in Philosophy 23. Stockholm: Almqvist and Wiksell.

Kulkarni, S. R., Lugosi, G., and Venkatesh, L. S. (1998). "Learning Pattern Classification: A Survey." *IEEE Transactions on Information Theory* 44: 2178–2206.

McDowell, J. (1998). *Mind, Value, and Reality*. Cambridge, Mass.: Harvard University Press.

Popper, K. (1979). *Objective Knowledge: An Evolutionary Approach*. Oxford: Clarendon Press.

Popper, K. (2002). *The Logic of Scientific Discovery*. London: Routledge. (Orig. published in German, 1934.)

Rawls, J. (1971). *A Theory of Justice*. Cambridge, Mass.: Harvard University Press.

Read, S. J., Snow, C. J., and Simon, D. (2003). "Constraint Satisfaction Processes in Social Reasoning." *Proceedings of the 25th Annual Conference of the Cognitive Science Society*: 964–969.

Redelmeier, D. A., and Shafir, E. (1995). "Medical Decision Making in Situations That Offer Multiple Alternatives." *Journal of the American Medical Association* 273: 302–305.

Rissanen, J. (1978). Modeling by Shortest Data Description. *Automatica* 14: 465–471.

Schwartz, B. (2004). *The Paradox of Choice: Why More Is Less*. New York: HarperCollins.

Simon, D. (2004). "A Third View of the Black Box." *University of Chicago Law Review* 71: 511–586.

Simon, D., and Holyoak, K. J. (2002). "Structural Dynamics of Cognition: From Consistency Theories to Constraint Satisfaction." *Personality and Social Psychology Review* 6: 283–294.

Simon, D., Pham, L. B., Le, Q. A., and Holyoak, K. J. (2001). "The Emergence of Coherence Over the Course of Decision Making." *Journal of Experimental Psychology: Learning, Memory, and Cognition* 27: 1250–1260.

Sinnott-Armstrong, W. (1999). "Varieties of Particularism." *Metaphilosophy* 30: 1–12.

Solomonoff, R. J. (1964). "A Formal Theory of Inductive Inference." *Information and Control* 7: 1–22, 224–254.

Stalker, D., editor (1994). *Grue! The New Riddle of Induction* Peru, Illinois: Open Court.

Stich, S., and Nisbett, R. (1980). "Justification and the Psychology of Human Reasoning." *Philosophy of Science* 47: 188–202.

Thagard, P. (1988). *Computational Philosophy of Science.* Cambridge, Mass.: MIT Press.

Thagard, P. (1989). "Explanatory Coherence." *Brain and Behavioral Sciences* 12: 435–467.

Thagard, P. (2000). *Coherence in Thought and Action.* Cambridge, Mass.: MIT Press.

Tversky, A., and Kahneman, D. (1974). "Judgment under Uncertainty: Heuristics and Biases." *Science* 185: 1124–1131.

Valiant, L. G. (1984). "A Theory of the Learnable." *Communications of the ACM* 27: 1134–1142.

Vapnik, V. (1979). *Estimation of Dependencies Based on Empirical Data.* (In Russian.) Moskow: Nauka. English translation (1982), New York: Springer. References are to the English translation.

Vapnik, V. (1998). *Statistical Learning Theory.* New York: Wiley.

Vapnik, V. (2000). *The Nature of Statistical Learning Theory*, second edition. New York: Springer.

Vapnik, V., and Chervonenkis, A. Ja. (1968). "On the Uniform Convergence of Relative Frequencies of Events to Their Probabilities." (In Russian.) *Doklady Akademii Nauk USSR* 181. Translated into English as "On the Uniform Convergence of Relative Frequencies of Events to Their Probabilities." *Theory of Probability and Its Applications* 16 (1971): 264–280. References are to the English translation.

Vapnik, V., and Chervonenkis, A. Ja. (1974). *Theory of Pattern Recognition*. (In Russian.) Nauka: Moscow.

Väyrynen, P. (2004). "Particularism and Default Reasons." *Ethical Theory and Moral Practice* 7: 53–79.

Wachowski, A., and Wachowski, L. (dir.) (1999). *The Matrix*. Warner Brothers.

Weston, J., Pèrez-Cruz, F., Bousquet, O., Chapelle, O., Elisseeff, A., and Schölkopf, B. (2003). "Feature Selection and Transduction for Prediction of Molecular Bioactivity for Drug Design." *Bioinformatics* 19: 764–771.

Wiggins, D. (1998). *Needs, Values, and Truth*, third edition. Oxford: Oxford University Press.

Index